AMERICAN CONSTITUTIONALISM ABROAD

Recent Titles in
Contributions to the Study of World History

Genocide and the Modern Age: Etiology and Case Studies of Mass Death
Isidor Wallimann and Michael N. Dobkowski, editors

Because They Were Jews: A History of Antisemitism
Meyer Weinberg

Societies in Upheaval: Insurrections in France, Hungary, and Spain in the Early Eighteenth Century
Linda Frey and Marsha Frey

The Practical Revolutionaries: A New Interpretation of the French Anarchosyndicalists
Barbara Mitchell

The Dragon and the Wild Goose: China and India
Jay Taylor

Land and Freedom: The Origins of Russian Terrorism, 1876–1879
Deborah Hardy

Young Guard! The Communist Youth League, Petrograd 1917–1920
Isabel A. Tirado

Engine of Mischief: An Analytical Biography of Karl Radek
Jim Tuck

Central America: Historical Perspectives on the Contemporary Crises
Ralph Lee Woodward, Jr., editor

The Free Germany Movement: A Case of Patriotism or Treason?
Kai P. Schoenhals

Victims and Survivors: Displaced Persons and Other War Victims in Viet-Nam, 1954–1975
Louis A. Wiesner

Tsar Paul and the Question of Madness: An Essay in History and Psychology
Hugh Ragsdale

The Orphan Stone: The Minnesinger Dream of Reich
Richard J. Berleth

American Constitutionalism Abroad

SELECTED ESSAYS IN COMPARATIVE CONSTITUTIONAL HISTORY

Edited by
GEORGE ATHAN BILLIAS

Contributions to the Study of World History, Number 16
JON L. WAKELYN, SERIES ADVISER

Greenwood Press
NEW YORK • WESTPORT, CONNECTICUT • LONDON

Library of Congress Cataloging-in-Publication Data

Billias, George Athan, 1919–
American constitutionalism abroad : selected essays in comparative constitutional history / George Athan Billias.
p. cm. — (Contributions to the study of world history, ISSN 0885-9159 ; no. 16)
Includes bibliographical references.
ISBN 0-313-26757-X (alk. paper)
1. United States—Constitutional law. 2. Constitutional history.
I. Title. II. Series.
KF4549.B9 1990
342.73'029—dc20
[347.30229] 89-27277

British Library Cataloguing in Publication Data is available.

Library of Congress Catalog Card Number: 89-27277
ISBN: 0-313-26757-X
ISSN: 0885-9159

First published in 1990

Greenwood Press, Inc.
88 Post Road West, Westport, Connecticut 06881

Printed in the United States of America

The paper used in this book complies with the Permanent Paper Standard issued by the National Information Standards Organization (Z39.48-1984).

10 9 8 7 6 5 4 3 2 1

Dedication

Truth is often stranger than fiction. This truism is illustrated by the tale of two men involved with this book. The first, Jacob Hiatt, was born and educated in Lithuania, and in the course of his university studies prepared a paper on the influence of the American Constitution. After graduating he began a career as district attorney and circuit court judge. In 1935 he fled from Lithuania to America to escape persecution at the hands of the Nazis, but his parents, who remained behind, perished tragically in the Holocaust.

Jacob Hiatt's continued thirst for knowledge brought him to Clark University where he studied under Professor Dwight E. Lee and received a master's degree in history in 1946. Entering the field of business, he became a highly successful industrialist. But he never forgot his American alma mater. In 1955 he was elected a Clark trustee, and dedicated his drive, intelligence, and means to many significant programs undertaken by the university. Among his numerous gifts, he endowed the Jacob and Frances Hiatt Chair in History in honor of his longtime mentor, Professor Lee.

The other man, editor of this volume, came to Clark in 1962. He had been a medical administrative officer with an armored division in the American army and, in the course of combat, evacuated victims who had survived the Holocaust. His shattering wartime experiences stirred him to study history and to become a university professor. Eventually his research interests in the influence of the American Constitution throughout the world led him to edit this book of collected essays.

In time the parallel lines in the lives of the two men converged. We met, became friends, served on Clark committees, and were elected together to other organizations. In 1983 the Clark History Department appointed me to the Jacob and Frances Hiatt Chair.

This book is affectionately dedicated, therefore, to Jack Hiatt—a magnificent human being, compassionate humanitarian, and concerned philanthropist—whom I love and admire. It is fitting that this particular volume with an international perspective bear his name: Jack himself has enriched the world in many ways. He has given generously of his time, energy, and resources to peoples and places scattered throughout the globe. With little regard to race, religion, or color, he has given to educational and cultural institutions, to deserving teachers and students, and to victims of disaster in different countries. Many of these acts of generosity were inspired by the memory of his parents and the loss of his beloved wife, Frances, who had shared his deep sympathies and sense of service. To him who has given much, much should be given in return. This book—a small gift to a great man—is given by one who understands that Jack deserves to be honored even more.

George Athan Billias
Jacob and Frances Hiatt Professor
of History, Emeritus

Contents

Acknowledgments

My thanks as editor go first and foremost to the contributors to this book for their essays. They showed great patience in putting up with my editorial demands and responded to criticisms and suggestions with a scholarly sense of responsibility. Without their cooperation, the publication of this volume in its present form would not have been possible.

Above and beyond my obligation to them, I have accumulated many specific debts that should be acknowledged. The greatest of these is to Lawrence W. Beer, Fred Morgan Kirby Professor of Civil Rights at Lafayette College. He read and commented on each of the essays, gave me the benefit of his scholarship in the field of comparative constitutional law in which he is an acknowledged authority, and provided me with wise counsel on this project throughout its development.

Walter Murphy of the Department of Politics at Princeton University played a different role—that of a gadfly. Although he disagreed with ideas expressed in several essays, his trenchant remarks proved most valuable. He is in no way responsible for the conclusions reached in the volume, but his constructive criticism helped to shape the outlines of the project in ways that even he was not aware.

Numerous other scholars—most of them historians—contributed to these essays in different ways. Gordon Wood provided a critique on a paper I delivered at the American Antiquarian Society in 1984 which caused me to rethink my approach and to write the essay that appears in these pages. Worcester colleagues at that time—Peter Onuf, Ronald Petrin, Robert Kolesar, Paul Lucas, and Robert Campbell—discussed my essay and deepened my understanding of this complex subject. Historians outside of Worcester—Gerald N. Grob, Milton M. Klein, Francis G. Couvares, Richard D. Brown, and Stanley Kutler—supplied useful suggestions and information. To Albert P. Blaustein at the Rutgers University Law School at Camden, I owe a special thanks for sharing with me certain essays on the influence of American constitutionalism abroad.

At Harvard University, I was given the privilege of using two libraries—Widener and the International Legal Studies Library—both of which provided materials I could not find elsewhere.

Members of the Clark University community, as always, were unfailingly generous with their support. At the Robert Hutchins Goddard Library, Susan Baughman, University Librarian, provided an environment conducive to scholarly research; Mary Hartman, Irene Walch, and Edward McDermott tracked down difficult references; and the entire staff was most cooperative despite my many requests. In Clark's secretarial pool—"Terry" Reynolds, Rene Baril, Virginia Chapman, and Krystin Sandberg—patiently typed and retyped the manuscript several times. Trudy Powers, our departmental secretary, came to my rescue on many critical occasions.

Financial support from sources both within and outside Clark University provided me the time to complete this project. A grant from the National Endowment for the Humanities (FA 26180–86) and the Exxon Educational Foundation were particularly helpful in this respect.

Finally, I've saved for last the person who deserves to be thanked first—my wife—Margaret Rose. Her love, warm understanding, and cheerful outlook worked wonders in sustaining my spirits. Equally important, she read the manuscript many times, counseled me, and insisted that every complexity be clearly expressed.

AMERICAN CONSTITUTIONALISM ABROAD

Introduction

George Athan Billias

American constitutionalism remains this country's greatest contribution to human freedom, the legitimation of slavery in the Constitution notwithstanding. It represents one of the most remarkable milestones in the history of Western constitutionalism. The ideas, ideals, and institutions of American constitutionalism have influenced different peoples in different lands over the past two hundred years. Foreign constitution-makers turned to features of American constitutionalism for models and examples, or were influenced by them in other ways when drafting their own instruments of government. American constitutionalism deserves to be ranked, therefore, alongside the other two major traditions of Western constitutionalism—those of Britain and France.

The definitive history of American constitutionalism abroad, however, remains to be written. To produce such a work would require legions of scholars, research over decades, and the mastery of the histories, languages, and customs of many countries throughout the globe. It would require also a discussion of the important contributions to American constitutionalism of British and French constitutionalism, as well as the impact of European Enlightenment ideas. This volume has a much more modest aim. It represents a pioneering effort in a largely unexplored field in the hope that these selected essays might stimulate other scholars to take up the more formidable task.

The best way to begin, perhaps, is to define two key terms employed in essays in this volume—"American constitutionalism" and "influence." "American historians tend to use... [constitutionalism] as a shorthand reference to the constitutional thought of the founding period," according to one authoritative source.[1] But constitutionalism also has a long tradition in Western history. It harks back to a problem that has plagued humanity since the days of ancient Greece and Rome: how to create government power capable of sustaining the stability and order required to realize the aims of a community, while at the same time defining and structuring that power in such a way as to prevent tyranny. The age-old search for the forms, procedures, and institutions most suitable for limiting power, on the one hand, and for promoting a community's sense of political right and justice, on the other, comprises the history of constitutionalism in Western thought.

American constitutionalism, for purposes of this volume, is defined as that complex of political concepts observable in certain constitutional documents, procedures, and institutions that came into being within the United States during the founding period from 1776 to 1791. This definition focuses, in part, upon six seminal documents written during this momentous decade and a half. This era represents the greatest creative period of constitutional thought in all of American history. Never again did American thinkers reach such heights in producing outstanding constitutional documents: the Declaration of Independence, the first state constitutions, the Articles of Confederation, the Federal Constitution, the *Federalist Papers*, and the Federal Bill of Rights.

These half-dozen documents by no means exhaust all the significant constitutional texts of the time. They represent, however, the ones viewed by foreign constitution-makers as comprising the principal elements of American constitutionalism. The concept of a "living constitution"—one that was constantly changing, developing, and reinterpreted—as exemplified by later court decisions, constitutional commentaries, and subsequent amendments, was often implied in both the form and spirit of the six documents. At the same time it may be said that these founding documents established the framework which limited the scope of possible future developments and additions in much the same way that the foundations of a house confine its superstructure.

Certain procedures and institutions established during the same formative years amounted to American constitutional innovations. Although not always completely original, they changed the entire course of Western constitutionalism. Three procedures—the custom of calling constituent constitutional conventions, the notion of resorting consistently to written constitutions, and the idea of ratification on a routine basis—were destined to become worldwide practices. Three institutions inherent or implied in the Federal Constitution—presidentialism, federalism, and what might be termed judicialism—were also emulated or discussed in many foreign constitutional conventions.

By tracing the influence of these documents, procedures, and institutions, and by analyzing how they were received and perceived by constitution-makers in other countries, it is possible to follow the spread of American constitutionalism throughout various parts of the world over time. Moreover, by breaking down United States constitutionalism into these component parts, the task of research becomes more manageable: traces of American constitutional practices are revealed in greater clarity, and instances where American ideals, ideas, and institutions provided inspiration become less ambiguous.

In comparing American constitutionalism with constitutional arrangements in other countries, scholars are well aware that written constitutions—even if declared fundamental law—by no means provide an accurate picture of the way power is exercised within a given country. Despite discrepancies between constitutional formulations and actual practices of government, however, the study of such documents is revealing and rewarding. Written constitutions provide an image, no matter how distorted and incomplete, of the institutions, practices, and procedures of governance. Even more important, written constitutions project ideals—as rulers (and sometimes the ruled) wish to have them understood.

When dealing with the spread of American constitutionalism, the term *influence* seems to be the most fitting to use. Scholars understand how imprecise and difficult it is to establish influence. Ideas, even misunderstood ideas, circulate quickly, mingle freely with ideas originating elsewhere, and become altered in transmission. But even if the results are sometimes elusive, they are nevertheless significant and worthy of study. *Influence* rather than *impact* is appropriate because it is a less restrictive term and implies indirect as well as direct interaction. Much of the influence of American constitutionalism was far less a case of cause and effect; it was more a matter of providing models, examples, and inspiration for foreign constitution-makers to discuss and debate.

In these essays, the term *influence* is used in two ways. It refers in some instances to situations where Americans provided a model to constitution-makers in other countries which were seeking to solve a specific problem. The reaction of these foreign constitution-makers was sometimes negative in nature. That is, they used an American constitutional feature as an anti-model in order to reject a proposed solution to some analogous problem. Influence is used in a second way to refer to those cases where foreign constitution-makers merely took into account America's constitutional ideas and experiences when discussing or framing their own instruments of government—whether they ultimately adopted American forms or not.

In tracing the worldwide influence of the six seminal documents, more is involved than simply examining their literary influence. Leaving aside for the moment the question of origins, the indisputable indebtedness to other countries, and the symbiotic relationship between European and American constitutionalism in the seventeenth and eighteenth centuries, these texts performed a variety of distinctive functions.

First, certain of these sources served to articulate what were viewed abroad as democratic American constitutional ideals. The Declaration of Independence is a case in point. This document often established a standard for certain democratically-inclined countries: their citizenry often insisted that their governments recognize the principle of equality before the law and that they guarantee individuals certain unalienable rights.

Second, certain procedures emerged in the writing and ratifying of these documents. One distinctive American contribution was the practice of committing constitutional principles to paper. The idea of a written constitution represented a giant step forward for Western constitutionalism. Although the United States did not produce the first written constitution in world history, America's resort to such a procedure launched the first great wave of written constitutions in modern history. The same can be said of the constituent constitutional convention. This kind of convention—incorporating the concept of popular sovereignty and subjecting civil authorities to the popular will—was introduced during the Revolutionary era. There were English origins for such an idea, but it never took hold and the constituent constitutional convention was first practiced in America. Without a doubt, this procedure remains America's most original political contribution to world history. The concept of a bill of rights was popularized during the same period. There were precedents for declarations of rights—in medieval times and in England in 1689, though the idea was not put into practice. But it was in late eighteenth-century America that the idea of appending a bill of rights to the constitution was first applied. This bill, or declaration, listed the rights of citizens on the one hand, and limited the power of the government over such rights on the other. France also shares in the bill of rights tradition because of its Declaration of the Rights of Man and the Citizen of 1789.

Finally, certain governmental institutions—legitimized either explicitly or implicitly in the Federal Constitution—were borrowed extensively by foreign constitution-makers. There were three such institutions, namely—presidentialism, federalism, and judicialism. Once again, these institutions were not entirely original, but constitution-makers elsewhere looked to the American example for practical experience.

America's framers, for example, created the presidency as an elected executive, granting him king-like powers to insure vigor and efficiency in government. But the president's powers were limited by a system of checks and balances and by the creation of separate institutions that shared governmental power. The presidency was adopted abroad far less than the other two features because of the lessons of history. After France's experience with Napoleon, European nations feared the idea of a man on horseback for the remainder of the nineteenth century. Following the Nazi-Fascist era, constitution-makers worried lest a strong leader like Hitler seize power and become a dictator. Certain countries adopted the institution of the American presidency, but adapted it to suit their own needs. Where presidentialism has been put into practice, a prime minister has sometimes been added, making the office of president more like a titular executive in a cabinet or parliamentary system than one similar to the American executive. In other instances, as in the case of Latin American countries, presidentialism assumed an exaggerated form—caudillismo or strongman rule—without the American system of checks and balances. But in both cases the origins of the institution can be traced clearly to the United States.

Of the three institutions, America's version of federalism drew the most interest. The Federal Constitution established a partnership of self-governing commonwealths with an elective central government powerful enough to promote and protect joint concerns. Tocqueville termed American federalism "a great discovery in modern political science." No other people had ever devised a federal structure for so large a territory with a republican central government. The American style of federalism offered a new solution to the age-old problem of reconciling legitimate local interests with the general good. It functions not only because of formal checks in the American Constitution but also because informal forces at work—religious, economic, and geographic—help to counterbalance one another. But American federalism is a dynamic concept: its definition has changed constantly, and in practice the division of governmental powers has shifted over time.

America's version of federalism or variations of it influenced several foreign countries in the nineteenth century. In Europe, Switzerland, Germany and Austria-Hungary were all affected to some degree. In Latin America, Argentina, Brazil, and Mexico adopted variants. The American version of federalism influenced constitution-makers in the British dominions of Canada, Australia, and South Africa, either in positive or negative terms. In the twentieth century, Britain transformed much of its empire into a commonwealth on somewhat the same basis. Federalism was also introduced into nearly a dozen countries in Europe, Asia, Latin America, and Africa. More importantly, the American principle of federalism caused statesmen to conceive of the same kind of federation along world lines—first in the League of Nations and then in the United Nations. Although member nations hardly exercised the powers American states had, the form of both organizations was similar to that of the American federal system.

If judicialism may be defined in a broad way as incorporating several elements—the doctrine of judicial review, guardianship of a constitution by the courts, the protection of human rights, and the citation of national court decisions as legal precedents in foreign courts—then a case can be made that American judicialism influenced countries in Europe, North America, South America and Asia. Allowances must be made, of course, for great differences: between common law and civil law countries; changes from natural law to positive law; and decentralized and centralized forms of judicial review. Keeping in mind these great differences, the American version of judicial review was tried at one time or another in the following countries—Argentina, Canada, Australia, India, Ireland, Greece, Norway, Denmark, Sweden, Switzerland, and post–World War II Germany and Italy. Since World War II, Germany, Italy, and several other countries have established courts to serve as guardians of their constitutions. The United States has had a long history of supporting the judicial protection of human rights both at home and abroad, even though it has yet to sign the 1948 United Nations Universal Declaration of Human Rights. Citation of American court decisions down through history has occurred in Argentina, Australia, Canada, the Philippine Islands, Ireland, Germany, and Japan.[2]

It is necessary, however, to keep in mind the dynamic changes that have taken place in these three institutional features over the course of American history. Presidentialism recently has become more prominent because of the greater significance of the office in foreign affairs, and the term "imperial presidency" reflects that change. Federalism remained an unresolved issue until the Civil War when the question of states' rights versus federal power was decided on the battlefield. The changes brought about by the outcome of the Civil War were institutionalized by the adoption of the Thirteenth, Fourteenth, and Fifteenth Amendments. They gave the federal government greater importance in defining common national goals—especially in the area of individual rights. The fact remains, however, that despite a century of centralization, existing state and local powers have not been eliminated and have even been reinforced under the current "new federalism." In the area of judicialism, the powers of the Supreme Court have also waxed and waned over time. *Marbury v. Madison* asserted the practice of self-legitimizing judicial review which had been implied in Article III of the Constitution. Congress reduced the Court's appellate jurisdiction, however, after the Civil War. The Court acquiesced in the *McCardle* decision—though not without pointing out that it might assert jurisdiction in certain cases. When the Warren Court inaugurated a new era of judicial activism a century later, it represented only one more shift in a long line of changes.

The essays that follow address a wide range of issues dealing with the influence of American constitutionalism abroad. Billias makes a case for the direct and indirect influence of American constitutionalism on Europe between two revolutionary eras—the American Revolution and the revolutions in Europe in 1848. Europe presents a particularly difficult analytical problem. Much of American constitutionalism was itself derived from European thought and experience in the first place. Billias traces the influence of the six founding documents in particular on European constitution-makers. He maintains that the Declaration of Independence broadened the claims of Americans from their rights as Englishmen to their rights as individuals. Americans thereby sounded the first call to cast constitutionalism in more universal terms. By appealing for the support of enlightened world opinion, the Declaration also linked the destiny of the new United States to countries bordering the Atlantic basin during the period which Robert R. Palmer has called "the age of the democratic revolution." The first American state constitutions likewise inaugurated a new era in constitution-making—they were responsible for popularizing the idea of a written constitution. The early state constitutions, the British heritage, and the French Declaration of 1789, all helped to spread the bill of rights tradition in Europe. The Articles of Confederation, America's first constitution, was cited as a model in the Dutch Republic in the 1770s as well as in Belgium in 1790. The Federal Constitution itself was imitated or cited more in Europe before 1848 than any other American constitutional document except, perhaps, for the Declaration. The *Federalist Papers* also influenced constitution-makers and thinkers—in France in the early 1790s, in Germany in the 1820s and in 1848, and in Switzerland in the 1830s and 1840s. Finally, the Federal Bill of Rights, the American state constitutions, the English Bill of Rights of 1689, and the French Declaration all helped to establish this particular tradition in a number of countries between 1776 and 1848. In their constitution-making during this period, Europeans borrowed from American procedures and institutions as well as from these half-dozen documents.

Latin America, next to Europe, presents the best case for tracing the influence of American constitutionalism abroad during the nineteenth century. Kolesar's essay demonstrates that North American constitutional documents sometimes served as models for certain Latin American countries. The appeal of the United States as a model was heightened by two considerations: the general anti-European tenor of the independence movement in Latin America, and a sense of common cause in Latin America with the former British colonies in North America. But Kolesar is quick to point out that the process of influence was hardly one of mere imitation. Indeed, he questions the degree of American influence, and in his intriguing title asks whether North American constitutionalism was a special lock which the keys of Latin America often failed to fit.

Latin Americans were cautious about applying North American constitutional principles. On the one hand, they often made significant modifications in North American constitutional features in order to accommodate them to their own political traditions. On the other hand, they resorted to North American constitutionalism for several reasons: they hoped to base their new nations on the same principles of the European Enlightenment, to create polities that would encourage social and economic development and thereby emulate the successful United States, and to break with certain historic strands of the Hispanic political tradition. Furthermore, the influence of North American constitutionalism in Latin America was affected by internal political and social conflicts within individual countries as well as by external relations between the two Americas.

The next essay in this volume differs from the others both in terms of its subject matter and its orientation. Peter and Nicholas Onuf are not interested, as are the other authors, in American constitutionalism abroad. They are concerned instead with analyzing America's efforts to influence the world more through international law. The Onufs argue that America's founding fathers hoped to bring about a more liberal world order based on peace and prosperity, but that they were less certain about doing so through constitutionalism than by other means. Americans saw themselves playing a more important role in world affairs by liberalizing and reforming practices in relations among nation-states: writing commercial treaties which would further the cause of both peace and prosperity, promoting alternatives to war by means of such measures as the arbitration movement, rationalizing such reforms by writing treatises, and codifying a regime of international law on a global basis. Within this context of liberalizing the world order, the Onufs discuss Henry Wheaton's classic treatise, *Elements of International Law*, and William Ladd's efforts to found an international peace movement.

Safran's essay is a well-defined case study of two European constitutions during the post–World War II period—the Bonn Constitution of 1949 and the French Constitution of 1958. He observes certain interesting parallels between these two documents and America's constitutional doctrines. But these intriguing resemblances, Safran notes, arose as the result of quite different circumstances. In the case of the democratic provisions of the Bonn Constitution of 1949, Safran describes a sharp debate over America's influence. Some scholars claim the West Germans deliberately followed American constitutionalism either because of the presence of the United States as an occupying power, or out of sincere admiration for American democracy. Other writers, however, point to influences closer to home: the Frankfurt Constitution of 1848–49, the Weimar Constitution of 1919, and the intense domestic reaction to the Nazi regime. If certain features in the French Constitution of 1958 resembled American constitutionalism, Safran concludes, they did so largely because French framers borrowed from earlier French constitutional models—such as the Constitutions of 1791 and 1848. These constitutions, in turn, were inspired by American examples or at least influenced by many of the same theories that had affected America's founding fathers.

The Asian continent remained unaffected by the influence of American constitutionalism until almost the end of the nineteenth century. The acquisition of the Philippines marked the beginning of direct American influence, but such influence remained confined largely to that colony until the end of World War II. The constitutional traditions of other Western colonizing powers—the British, French, Dutch, and German—as well as indigenous constitutional practices played a far more important role in that part of the world. American constitutionalism was only of occasional or minor significance in the period before 1945.

Beer's essay notes the different modes of American constitutional influence in Asia since 1945. One form of influence became evident as Asian constitution-makers took into account certain of the six seminal American documents—such as the Declaration and the Federal Constitution. A second form of influence occurred as the result of Asian consultation with American experts in drawing up, revising, or amending constitutions. A third resulted from a greater awareness of American constitutional values as Asian leaders became exposed to them in the world press, in other mass media, or at Western educational institutions. And a fourth came as the result of the adoption of the American version of judicial review.

The Asian countries affected most, according to Beer, were Japan, the Philippines, South Korea, and India. Japan represents the most outstanding example of American constitutional influence not only in Asia but for the entire twentieth century. American officials in the occupation force after World War II presumably prepared much of the Japanese Constitution of 1947 and incorporated in it many features of American constitutionalism. Japanese judges, moreover, often studied precedents established by the United States Supreme Court in constitutional cases and referred to them in their decisions. Important Japanese legal scholars also kept abreast of American laws and judicial decisions that affected constitutional matters and cited them frequently.

When the Philippines came under American colonial rule, the United States sought to institutionalize a system of democratic law. With the granting of independence to the Philippines in 1946 (as promised in 1934), the constitution that was approved by the Filipinos and Americans became the supreme law of the land. The Constitution of 1935 incorporated many fundamental principles of American constitutionalism—the separation of powers, judicial review, a bill of rights, and due process—and it remained in force until 1972. But these principles were disregarded when the regime of Ferdinand Marcos imposed martial law in that year and proclaimed a new constitution in 1973. Other authoritarian constitutional features were introduced in 1981 and 1984 and continued until the fall of the Marcos government in 1986. The 1987 Philippine Constitution, ratified by plebiscite, returned many of the former features.

The role of Americans in framing South Korea's constitutions was less important and more indirect than in the case of Japan and the Philippines. Throughout that country's turbulent history, however, the United States exercised considerable influence on Korean constitutional developments: by imposing political pressure on Korean presidents engaged in anticonstitutional practices, by withholding economic aid in certain situations, and by educating Koreans in American constitutional values both at home and in the United States.

India's Constitution of 1950 was also influenced by American practices. The concept of judicial review was one such example—though this feature stemmed as well from British precedents. The phrasing of the due process clause in the Indian Constitution was borrowed directly from the American-influenced Japanese Constitution of 1947. More significantly, Indian constitution-makers consulted with American presidents, jurists, and legislators before they wrote their document.

This book, at bottom, is asking a broad question: how do constitutional ideas, ideals, and institutions travel across geographic and cultural borders? In the case of these essays, the choice of countries or regions examined is necessarily selective in that it reflects the interests and expertise of the individual contributors. Not all the authors, it should also be noted, emphasize the importance of the six founding documents. And the essays reflect the different methodological and disciplinary approaches of the contributors.

The case made for the spread of American constitutionalism in these essays calls for certain caveats. First, it is clear that a majority of the world's constitutions were *not* influenced by American constitutionalism. Many countries looked mainly to the French Revolution and to subsequent French experiences in constitution-making. Other nations relied upon Britain's Westminster model or even more on the Whitehall model that was created to grant independence to countries that were once part of the British empire. There were, in addition, certain key constitutions that provided precedents for other countries: the Spanish Constitution of 1812, the Belgian Constitution of 1831, the Constitution of Imperial Germany of 1871, the Mexican Constitution of 1917, and constitutions based on different Soviet models. In many Asian countries the constitutional traditions of the former mother country left an impact: French constitutionalism on what is now Vietnam, Kampuchea, and Laos; British constitutionalism on India, Burma, many South Asian territories, Malaysia, and Singapore; Dutch constitutionalism on the Dutch East Indies, now Indonesia; and Japanese constitutionalism on Korea. In Africa the same was true of countries formerly controlled by France, Britain, Germany, and Belgium. The political world, therefore, is hardly American constitutionalism writ large.

Second, all constitutions by their nature are mostly indigenous. They should and often do reflect the specific needs, hopes, and desires of the peoples for whom they were written or framed. No country, as a result, rigidly tried to superimpose American constitutionalism as a blueprint upon its people. When American constitutional ideas, ideals, and institutions were emulated, they were changed and used in far different ways than they had been during America's formative period.

Third, the influence of American constitutionalism—a model at times, an inspiration at other times—was often indirect rather than direct. Many countries were eclectic when borrowing from foreign constitutional models, thus making it difficult to trace constitutional precedents directly to any single source. The Belgian Constitution of 1831 provides a case in point. Although the Belgians borrowed certain features from American constitutionalism, they relied much more upon French precedents. The Belgian Constitution, in turn, was widely emulated by a number of European countries throughout the nineteenth century. America's influence, therefore, was not only transmitted indirectly but also blended with other constitutional traditions. The result has been the spread only of traces of American constitutionalism throughout the world rather than any straightforward duplication of American constitutional structures.

Finally, American constitutional principles and practices were transformed when transplanted to foreign soil. The American style of federalism, for example, assumed a different form when exported abroad. Switzerland, which followed the American model most closely, developed a federal system that had its own history and operates quite differently in many particulars. The same was true of American presidentialism and judicialism as noted previously.

But this is not to say that American constitutionalism, while transformed when transplanted, was without influence. Chinese students demonstrating in Beijing in May 1989 could be heard chanting slogans from three of America's seminal constitutional documents—the Declaration, the *Federalist Papers*, and the Bill of Rights. Such slogans were not mere rhetoric. Some scholars would argue that, when used in a foreign context, such American constitutional ideas had little or no meaning and lacked any intellectual force. This is to miss the point. People live by myths, are stirred to action by slogans, and are inspired by models and examples. Wherever issues of popular democracy and liberty are at stake in any part of the world, there the concepts of American constitutionalism and the winged words of America's founding fathers are destined to be recalled.

What does this volume have to do with the main outlines of American history and with the foreign perception of how America has related to the rest of the world? Americans have always prided themselves on being a pragmatic people. The world appears to have perceived the American people in much the same light, as a people who generally placed less emphasis upon ideas and more upon material matters. The world seems to have valued the United States most for its material goods—for American manufactured products, agricultural crops, and technological improvements. But perhaps we are, after all, a more ideologically minded people than we realize, as clearly reflected in the concepts—constitutional concepts—which we have given to other peoples of the world.

NOTES

1. Leonard Levy et al., *The Encyclopedia of the American Constitution*, 4 vols. (New York: Macmillan Company, 1986), 2:473.

2. Mauro Cappelletti, *Judicial Review in the Contemporary World* (Indianapolis: Bobbs-Merrill Company, 1971), 47, 59, 69, 75ff. Judicial review has made great strides since World War II.

1

American Constitutionalism and Europe, 1776–1848

George Athan Billias

George Athan Billias emphasizes all three aspects of American constitutionalism—documents, procedures, and institutions—and their effect on Europe between the American Revolution and the European revolutions of 1848. He stresses the influence of six founding documents—the Declaration of Independence, the first state constitutions, the Articles of Confederation, the Federal Constitution, the *Federalist Papers*, and the Federal Bill of Rights—on the Old World in this period. At the same time, he underlines the importance of three American procedures—the calling of a constituent constitutional convention, the requirement that a constitution be written, and the ratification of the constitution by the constituents—as they were adopted or adapted in Europe. Finally, he shows how three institutions inherent or implied in the Federal Constitution—presidentialism, the American version of federalism, and what he terms judicialism—affected Europe from 1776 to 1848.

American constitutionalism—if defined in terms of the constitutional documents, procedures, and institutions that came into being during the founding period from 1776 to 1791—represents a landmark in world history and in Western constitutionalism.[1] The principles and practices of American constitutionalism created in these fifteen years have influenced countries the world over for the past two centuries. Foreign constitution-makers turned to United States constitutionalism for models, or they were influenced by American constitutional features in other ways when drafting their own documents. This crucial decade and a half marked a major turning point in the history of Western constitutionalism. The world was never the same, constitutionally speaking, after 1776.

American constitutionalism had its greatest impact on Europe between the American Revolution and the European revolutions of 1848. The focus on Europe during this period is particularly appropriate. There existed a symbiotic relationship between Europe and America as the American and French revolutions launched a new era of written constitutions at the end of the eighteenth century. Robert R. Palmer has justifiably named this entire period "the age of the democratic revolution."[2] The influence of American constitutionalism on Europe during this age was quite different from that in subsequent years; the United States was then a small and less important member in the world community. Its constitutional influence was relatively "pure," so to speak, being based mainly upon the intrinsic appeal it held for contemporary constitution-makers. After the turn of the twentieth century, however, the influence of American constitutionalism was affected by the status of the United States as a world power, mother country, and victor in two global wars.

The six founding documents written during America's early years—the Declaration of Independence, first state constitutions, Articles of Confederation, Federal Constitution, *Federalist Papers*, and Federal Bill of Rights—clearly influenced European constitutionalism from 1776 to 1848. Other documents could be considered, but these half-dozen texts undoubtedly had the greatest effect. Two questions about them are appropriate. When were these documents first reprinted, translated, and discussed in the countries of Europe? And what evidence was there of any American constitutional influence—direct or indirect—in terms of enunciating ideals, copying procedures, or creating institutions in these countries?

The origins of American constitutionalism drew not only from American experience but from three streams of thought flowing from Europe to America: the heritage of Western civilization, the European Enlightenment, and the British constitutional tradition. Being transplanted Europeans, Americans were profoundly affected by the long-standing constitutional traditions of the Western world. Americans derived their constitutional ideas from the same antecedents as Europeans: religious attitudes stemming from the Judeo-Christian tradition, ideas derived from the constitutions of classical antiquity in Greece and Rome, constitutional theories developed by thinkers in the medieval period, and ideas revived in the Renaissance by writers like Machiavelli. American constitutionalism, therefore, must always be viewed against the backdrop of Western constitutionalism as a whole.

Americans were influenced also by the ideas of the European Enlightenment. Some historians hold that the Enlightenment was a transatlantic movement and that men like Benjamin Franklin, Thomas Jefferson, and John Adams contributed ideas as well as receiving them. These Americans, like Europeans, shared the Enlightenment notion that the universe was rational, ordered, and coherent, and best understood by means of natural laws. Both believed that mankind was one: that men everywhere were subject alike to the same laws, motivated by the same passions, and entitled to the same rights. They believed in the power of reason: that reason could create universal laws, achieve ends that reason dictated as just, and that reason would make men and nations follow laws that were sound. Generally speaking, they were interested in improving human life on earth with as many reforms as possible. Some of the more romantic even believed that such reforms would lead to the perfectability of man.

The main difference between the European and American Enlightenment was crucial: Americans were in a better position than Europeans to put their ideas into practice and to translate their ideals into reality. They did not have to cope with the conservative institutions of feudal Europe that resisted change—an aristocratic ruling class, an established church, and a national army. One scholar, in fact, portrayed the Federal Constitution essentially as Enlightenment ideas being put into practice.[3]

The British constitutional tradition was likewise part of America's intellectual heritage from the Old World. Like other Englishmen, American colonists believed the British Constitution to be the best in the world—at least until the ostensible violations prior to the Revolution. They were proud of the British Constitution because it protected the lives, liberties, and property of its subjects better than any empire on earth. They gloried in their "rights as Englishmen"—of due process of law, of trial by jury, of exemption from taxation except by vote of elected representatives, and to petition for a redress of grievances. Americans were proud too of the representative nature of English government and of the fact that it followed the principle of limited government. Such British constitutional rights were guaranteed to the colonists in their colonial charters.

Americans were affected as much by their experience as colonists over a century and a half as by ideas. Puritanism with its emphasis on the idea of a voluntary compact or covenant among like-minded religious believers helped to shape their concept of secular government as a social contract. Americans identified the covenants they formed in establishing governments with the concept of a social contract expounded by John Locke and by French philosophers. Men supposedly were not content to live in a barbaric state of nature without law and order; they consented in accepting defined rules of government. Their participation in society constituted a social contract between the rulers and the ruled in which both parties abided by their prescribed roles. The rulers ruled in a responsible manner, and the ruled were obedient and deferred to them. If the rulers proved to be irresponsible and abused their trust, the ruled could break the contract. Americans tended to view all governments as resting on such agreements. The colonial charters, or constitutions, of each colony were viewed as social contracts between the Crown and the colonies.

American experience with English political institutions likewise helped to form the basis of the American constitutional tradition. The structure of government was roughly the same in most colonies—governor, council, and legislature—with some exceptions. But with the passage of time, the legislative branch achieved supremacy over the others. The colonies, as a result, gained a considerable measure of self-government over their internal affairs.

The colonies at the same time fit within the structure of the British empire. They represented part of an interlocking system where final legal authority over imperial matters was located in London. The government of the empire was federal in structure, loosely speaking, and many Americans believed that the power to govern was divided into two spheres. The central government in London exercised a large measure of centralized control over imperial affairs, while the colonial governments felt they had control over many internal matters. The system was ill-defined, cumbersome, and sometimes unworkable. Americans, nevertheless, had had practical experience with the concept of federalism before the coming of the Revolution.

Finally, American colonists had been deeply influenced by the republican ideology that formed part of the British tradition of constitutionalism. A republic could be distinguished from other societies by virtue of its purpose as well as its form of government. Where other states sought to further the interests of their kings or other groups that controlled them, the aim of a republic was to advance the common interests of its people. Republicanism required not only popular political institutions but virtuous citizens. Such citizens theoretically would forego their selfish, private interests for the good of society as a whole.

Republicanism and the republican tradition stretched back to the classical times of Greece and Rome. The tradition had been revived by Renaissance thinkers like Machiavelli, and a Puritan republic had actually been established briefly in England in the seventeenth century. During the late seventeenth and early eighteenth centuries, radical Whig thinkers in England had developed an antiauthoritarian position against the British establishment based upon republican ideas. This English Whig ideology—which emphasized an eternal struggle between power and liberty as reflected in the battles between executive and legislative institutions—influenced Americans deeply.

Many American revolutionaries became convinced that liberty was fleeing the corrupt monarchical society of England to seek asylum in America. In America the people were presumed to be more virtuous and republican-minded. Republicanism increasingly served as a radicalizing ideology during the Revolution. Many Americans came to believe their destiny was to erect a new republic—one dedicated to the ideas of popular government and the principles of liberty. This republican ideology, when coupled with the Christian evangelical millennial ideas regarding the imminent second coming of Christ, infused Americans with a messianic sense of mission. Americans began viewing themselves as God's chosen people with a special mission in history: their role was to lead the world toward a new golden age of greater human freedom and Christian righteousness.[4]

With this brief background, it is possible to examine more clearly the influence of the six founding documents under consideration. American constitutionalism consisted of principles, ideas, and political mechanisms that were quite distinguishable from their European counterparts. What Americans did was to take principles Europeans had subscribed to for centuries and to translate them into practical ideas and governmental institutions. Once established in America, many of these ideas and institutions soon spread to other parts of the world.

THE DECLARATION OF INDEPENDENCE

The Declaration ranks in the eyes of most foreigners as the most important public paper ever published in the United States. Besides being the nation's birth certificate, it represents the best expression of America's constitutional values. Many American lawyers and legal scholars, however, do not consider the Declaration a constitutional document; in their eyes it lacks the force of a legal instrument associated with constitutions. They perceive it instead as a hortatory document; it proclaims rights but is not a constitutional document that creates a government which grants or guarantees such rights. Four counter arguments suggest that the Declaration may indeed be considered a constitutional document.

First, other nations probably identify American constitutionalism with the Declaration more than with any other single document. Peoples throughout the world consider it to be one of the great written charters of human freedom and an even more important constitutional document than the Federal Constitution itself. This was so because the Declaration embodied a statement of principles basic to American constitutionalism: that all men were created equal or were equal by nature, that they had a right to life and to enjoy liberty and pursue happiness, that just government should rest upon the consent of the governed, and that when government became destructive of such ends men had a right to alter or abolish it. The Declaration was seen as a symbol, namely, the opening statement of a new age of constitutional reform. In this new age, men everywhere would throw off the fetters of tyranny and arbitrary rule to embrace liberty, self-government, and the ideal of republicanism.

The Declaration reputedly had almost no influence abroad immediately following the Revolution; Europeans scarcely mentioned it at that time.[5] But the famous preamble subsequently exercised a powerful effect not only throughout Europe but in other parts of the globe. "During the nineteenth century," wrote Carl Becker, "it was accepted by radical and revolutionary parties in every European country, in South America and in the United States as a classic formulation of the fundamental democratic doctrines that governments derive 'their just Powers from the consent of the governed,' and that when 'any form of Government becomes . . . destructive of the natural rights of man it is the Right of the People to alter or to abolish it.' "[6]

Second, the Declaration can qualify as a constitutional document because it represented the concept of the social contract. In the minds of many Americans in 1776, the Declaration symbolized the precise moment when the social contract between Britain and the thirteen colonies was dissolved. Since the British Constitution supposedly had been subverted by the king, the original contract between the monarch and the American people was broken. The colonists, according to this theory, were no longer obliged to be obedient to George III. The Declaration, in other words, represented an attempt to put into practice in a literal way the severing of the contract between ruler and ruled.

The Declaration, more importantly, served to provide the constitutional basis for creating new social contracts in the form of state governments. The state constitutions written during and after 1776 were regarded as social contracts; they allowed governments to be established on the state level based on the constituent power of the people. In the wake of the Declaration, America's founding fathers, therefore, fell back upon the contract theory to provide a warrant for erecting new state governments.[7]

Finally, the principles of the Declaration itself were incorporated into a number of the first state constitutions. The spirit as well as actual phrases of the Declaration were written into the preambles of eight state constitutions. In the case of New York, the connection was even more pronounced: the entire Declaration was incorporated into the first constitution of 1777.[8] Hence through the medium of the state constitutions, the principles of the Declaration were widely disseminated throughout Europe during the last quarter of the eighteenth century.

THE FIRST STATE CONSTITUTIONS

America's first state constitutions, because of their availability, exercised the greatest influence on Europe in the period between the American and French revolutions. Written between 1776 and 1782, these documents inaugurated a new era in Western constitutionalism. Within a single year—1776—eight new state constitutions were written and adopted and two others modified. "That year," wrote constitutional scholar Benjamin Wright, "must therefore rank with 1787 as one of the two most significant years in the history of modern constitution-making."[9]

Despite their significance, these key documents were often overlooked. Robert R. Palmer chastised his colleagues for not including them in a symposium in 1973 devoted to the key testaments of the American Revolution. Viewed from a comparative perspective, Palmer noted, the first state constitutions deserved to be ranked alongside such famous documents as the Declaration and Articles of Confederation. "These state constitutions," Benjamin Wright wrote, "were the most advanced, by far the most democratic, in the world at that time."[10]

Within the context of Western constitutional history, the state constitutions held great significance by virtue of the fact they were written. Countries had issued occasional documents of constitutional import over the ages, but it was not until the seventeenth century that a few scattered written constitutions began to appear. With the adoption of the American state constitutions in the 1770s, however, a new age of written constitutions was born. Written constitutions followed in France in the 1790s, as well as in those countries affected by the French Revolution. After centuries of relative inactivity, country after country in Europe and Latin America suddenly began to alter their constitutional traditions. More often than not that change began with a call for a written constitution. A veritable epidemic of constitution-writing broke out.[11]

The American innovation of a constituent constitutional assembly likewise occured first on the state level. The precedent set by Massachusetts in calling a special assembly in 1780 to frame a constitution quickly took hold in France. Brissot de Warville, political leader in the French Revolution, argued in 1789 that the Estates General could not draw up a constitution; only a constitutional convention had such authority. "We owe its discovery to the Free Americans," he said, "and this device of the Free Americans can perhaps be very easily adapted to the circumstances in which France now finds itself."[12] Constitutional conventions or constituent assemblies were used throughout the era of the French Revolution in Europe and later in other countries in different parts of the world to frame constitutions when older institutions had been superseded by revolution or other means.

The American idea of ratifying a written constitution, which originated in the state of Massachusetts in 1780, soon was also adopted in Europe. In France, for example, the Constitution of 1793 was submitted to the people who accepted it overwhelmingly 1,801,908 to 11,610. The French went further in this regard than the Americans, who had not offered the Federal Constitution for direct popular ratification. Two years later, the French Constitution of 1795 was ratified by the French nation voting on terms that approximated universal manhood suffrage.[13]

The first state constitutions, moreover, symbolized the change from monarchical rule to republicanism which influenced Europe during "the age of the democratic revolution." Republics were a form of government known throughout history to be fragile and unstable. According to Montesquieu and other theorists, republics to be successful had to meet two conditions: to be small in size and to encompass a homogeneous population. The only existing republics in Europe at the time of the American Revolution—Holland and several Italian and Swiss city-states—met those criteria. When the American states wrote their constitutions, they incorporated distinctly republican features: the rights and liberties of the people were spelled out, legislatures were no longer bound by obnoxious restraints except those imposed by the people, and governors were shorn of much of their power.

The effect of the state constitutions was immediate and widespread. In France they became extremely important in the years just prior to the French Revolution. "They clarified and formulated the very thoughts that the French themselves entertained," concluded Palmer.[14] American state constitutions were published five times in France in the decade following 1776. They were discussed and commented upon by leading French intellectuals—Condorcet, Duc de la Rochefoucald, Turgot, and Demeunier. John Adams and John Stevens wrote books or pamphlets on state constitutions, and their translated works became the center of controversy among French constitutional theorists. On the floor of the French Assembly in 1789, references to the documents were on the lips of scores of speakers.[15] Although there were numerous reasons entirely indigenous to France for an insistence upon written constitutions, the concrete example provided by the Americans, without doubt, stimulated the French to take this striking step.

The American influence of one state constitution—that of Virginia and its Declaration of Rights of 1776—upon the famous French Declaration of the Rights of Man of 1789 has long been debated by scholars.[16] Thomas Jefferson, when in Paris, discussed the Virginia Declaration with Lafayette, who, in turn, proposed a plan for a French bill of rights. Delegates to the French National Assembly in 1789 were already familiar with the Virginia precedent. But most scholars believe it was the concrete actions taken in America—the notion of a numbered list, its promulgation, and its attachment to a written constitution—that were important rather than the American ideas in the document itself. When comparing the two documents, scholars observed great parallels: the sequence in which ideas were presented was almost identical; the general notions of natural and civil rights were nearly the same; and the affirmation of the equality of men, the securing of all men's rights to life, liberty, and property, and the doctrine of popular sovereignty were quite similar. But there were differences in substance as well, arising from the different institutional settings within the two countries. The French Declaration went further: it was more universal in its appeal to all mankind, its declaration of rights was more abstract, and its ideas of national sovereignty more concise. The documents were so closely intertwined, however, as to be almost indistinguishable. Both were inspired by the same theories, and many American ideas that ultimately reached France were based on French Enlightenment ideas in the first place. In terms of providing precedents to other countries, the American and French declarations should be considered part of a combined American-French constitutional tradition—it is impossible to leave out these two antecedents in modern history.

The American state constitutions, coupled with Thomas Paine's writings, were destined to become the very symbol of an eighteenth-century revolution. With the French armies spreading such notions of constitutionalism, six revolutionary regimes were set up by 1799 as republics: the Batavian, Helvetic, Cisalpine, Ligurian, Roman, and Neapolitan republics. Like America and France, each issued a written constitution, each had a declaration of rights, and each proclaimed the people to be sovereign.[17]

Belgium was also influenced by the first state constitutions and other American documents. When the Belgian revolt against the Hapsburg monarchy first broke out in 1789, the province of Flanders resorted to phrases from the Declaration of Independence to proclaim its freedom. Then in 1790 the democratic party in Belgium considered casting the new government along the lines set forth in the American state constitutions that had been published in the provinces. The Belgian republic proved short-lived, however, and these plans were never put into effect.[18]

In the Netherlands the influence of the first state constitutions was even more pronounced. By 1781 a translation of all the recently drafted constitutions of the thirteen states had become available. John Adams, minister to Holland, helped to disseminate American constitutional ideas and documents. His close association with Jan Luzac resulted in the first European translation of the Massachusetts Constitution of 1780. Information regarding American constitution-making gained wide notice also through Johan Derk Van der Capellen—leader of the Patriot cause who ordered the Declaration of Independence translated into Dutch and who personally translated the Massachusetts Constitution. As a result the Dutch became more familiar with the language of representative democracy and began to identify the American Revolution more closely with their own nationalist cause.[19]

Dutch use of American constitutional documents helped to sharpen the political debate in Holland. Van der Capellen drew on his knowledge of American constitutional documents to move the debate for independence closer to one based on natural rights rather than historical arguments. The Dutch Patriot movement thus came to resemble the American pattern which had also begun by using theories about the historical rights of Englishmen and then moved to a justification of revolution based on natural rights.

The influence of the American example is evident also in the Leyden Draft—a revolutionary manifesto issued by the Patriots in 1785—as well as in the Declaration presented to the States of Holland in 1787. The Leyden Draft contained a number of ideas comparable to those found in American sources: a definition of liberty as an inalienable right, the idea of popular sovereignty, the right of free speech, and ideas of religious toleration. This manifesto turned out to be an early ancestor of the democratic constitution adopted in Holland after 1848.[20] The Dutch historian Jan de Witt insisted that the Declaration of 1787 embodied American influences. "Although these demands arose in the first place out of Dutch conditions," he wrote, "the influence of the American [state] constitutions is visible in it.... Especially the constitution of Massachusetts, drafted by Adams himself, had made a strong impression in the Netherlands."[21] Although the Patriot revolt was crushed in 1787, and the Batavian republic which emerged in the 1790s owed much more to French constitutional influences, American constitutional ideas continued to exercise some influence in Holland.

The Norwegian Constitution of 1814 was also directly influenced by the American state constitutions. One of the delegates to the constituent assembly convened at Eidsvold brought a copy of the French translation of the American state constitutions, whose publication Benjamin Franklin had arranged in 1783. A draft of the Eidsvold Constitution contained a direct translation of Article 30 of the Massachusetts Constitution, dealing with the principle of the separation of powers.[22]

When beginning their struggle for independence, Greek revolutionaries in the Messina assembly observed that it was the Americans who first proclaimed "the rights to which all men are by nature equally entitled." After the Greek Declaration of Independence, the Constitution of Troezen was eventually adopted in 1827. This charter of Hellenic liberties contained many constitutional features which, though not solely American, were partially inspired by the example of the United States: the doctrine that government should rest on the consent of the people, the principle of equality before the law, the idea of freedom of speech, safeguards against arbitrary taxation, and protection against imprisonment without due process of law. Several of these provisions grew out of an exchange of letters between the Greek patriot Adamantios Korais and Thomas Jefferson, who suggested that the state constitutions rather than the Federal Constitution might serve as better models for the Greeks.[23]

The affinity between European revolutionaries and the first state constitutions could even be found in faraway Russia. Alexander Radishchev, sometimes called the first Russian revolutionary, wrote a book in 1790 entitled *A Journey from St. Petersburg to Moscow.* In it he quoted the American state constitutions and their declaration of rights in order to criticize the oppressive institutions of Russia. Disliking Radishchev's radical ideas, the Russian ruler had him exiled to Siberia as an example to other subversives.[24]

By the mid-nineteenth century, however, the influence of American state constitutions abroad had diminished sharply. The Federal Constitution increasingly became the model that foreign countries looked to. During the Civil War, moreover, the Federal Constitution emerged triumphant in the power struggle with the state constitutions. By this time as well, these constitutions had become too specific and detailed in form to serve as examples to foreigners. Despite their later decline in importance, however, the influence of the first state constitutions in Europe had been truly remarkable during the early years of the republic.

THE ARTICLES OF CONFEDERATION

The Articles of Confederation, the first constitution of the United States, has had a poor reputation among most American historians. Scholars for the most part have been ahistorical and guilty of presentism. Instead of studying the document in its proper historical context, they have accepted uncritically the arguments of the Federalists seeking to replace it. Thus the much-maligned Articles served as a stalking horse: its weaknesses were magnified to glorify the strengths of the much-admired Federal Constitution.

One need not go so far as the late Merrill Jensen, who argued that the Articles could conceivably have served as America's constitution had it not been undermined by the Federalists.[25] Taken on its own merits, however, the Articles had much to recommend it. The document marked a promising beginning of a new form of federalism. It acknowledged the sovereignty of the states, and, at the same time, limited that sovereignty by setting up a separate central government. Most important of all, it made "a start in the direction of constitutional federalism under which the government is that of individuals," according to one authority.[26]

The structure of government itself under the Articles was more constitutionally sound than is generally acknowledged. The framers of the Federal Constitution adopted many principles and provisions of the Articles; numerous powers given to Congress and some restraints imposed upon the states were carried over from the Articles to the new Constitution. Certainly the Articles proposed in 1777 and approved in 1781 continued the trend toward republicanism—in the direction of liberty and away from authority—begun by the first state constitutions.

The Articles served also as a model for constitution-makers and intellectuals in Europe. Between the American and French Revolutions, French intellectuals in particular held the Articles in high esteem. Indeed, the document was published more widely in France between 1776 and 1783 than either the Declaration of Independence or the state constitutions.[27]

When the Belgians adopted an Act of Union in 1790, it was modelled in part after the Articles of Confederation and occasionally repeated the same phrases. It is safe to assume, therefore, that the Belgians had a copy of the document. The new United States of Belgium, in fact, also called their governing body a "Congress." But the Belgian situation cannot be equated with the American example too much. In Belgium it was the conservative wing of the anti-Austrian revolt (those hoping to maintain nobles, clergy, and town notables in their positions after the Austrians were driven out) who supported the loose and decentralized union of the Articles. In America it was the other way around: the emphasis on states' rights was supported by the forces that were presumably more popular and democratic.[28]

In Holland Pieter Paulus, a brilliant young lawyer writing a major study on the Union of Utrecht in the 1770s, asserted that the Dutch Union served as a shining example of the Articles of Confederation which had just been published. Paulus cited the complete text of the Articles, praised the as-yet unratified document, and concluded that it was almost as perfect as the Union of Utrecht. Soon, however, he changed his mind. He came to believe that the loose federal system in the Netherlands would lead to its downfall in his lifetime—which indeed it did.[29]

THE FEDERAL CONSTITUTION

The Federal Constitution—the world's oldest written national constitution—has obviously been a most important model for foreign constitution-makers. Its main features were imitated in Europe during the years from 1776 to 1848 more than any other constitutional document (with the possible exception of the Declaration of Independence). Several key features from the Federal Constitution served most consistently as models for European constitution-makers during this period. They included the following: the idea of presidentialism, the American version of federalism, the American style of judicial review, the introduction of the concept of popular sovereignty into specific constitutional provisions, the notion of checks and balances, and the doctrine of the separation of powers.

Extreme care must be taken, however, in attributing these general European developments to direct American influence. The doctrine of the separation of powers is a case in point. In America this doctrine had specific historical antecedents, including the experience derived from colonial charters as well as theories advanced by Montesquieu and Locke. Montesquieu, it was believed at the time, put forward the theory that the government should be divided into executive, legislative, and judicial functions and that each should be allocated to a separate individual or group in order to achieve a balancing of power. To many Americans this came to mean, among other things, that there should be separate executive, legislative, and judicial branches, each acting as a check or balance against the others. To this theory were added the ideas of bicameralism and a strong executive to provide for additional checks and balances. In France these American precedents failed to fit the needs of the French. The most important barrier to the creation of a bicameral legislature was the fear that an upper house would tend to protect and perpetuate the French aristocracy by giving the upper class a specific constitutional role. To some Frenchmen the idea of a strong executive carried with it the threat of arbitrary government and tyranny. Nor did all the French necessarily view the doctrine of the separation of powers through the eyes of Montesquieu, according to some French constitutional scholars.[30]

Some members of the French Constitutional Assembly of 1789 cited the American precedent in favor of a two-house legislature and the doctrine of balance of powers. Eventually, however, the more radical Jacobins argued against the American system. They favored a unitary legislature with no constitutional place for the aristocracy. In the end the radicals prevailed. Generally speaking, they anticipated the tendency of European democratic factions to favor centralized governments, single-house legislatures, and weak executives.

The French Constitution of 1791, to be specific, more than all the other French constitutions written in the 1790s, most closely paralleled the Federal Constitution. There were provisions for a more rigorous separation of power between the executive and legislature—including a reference to the incompatibility of national executive and legislative offices, for extreme administrative decentralization, and for freedom of religion. The 1791 Constitution stipulated, moreover, that ministers were to be chosen by the chief executive (the king) and be answerable to him and not to the parliament. Finally, the document proclaimed that all citizens were equal before the law but showed an even greater awareness of social rights than the Federal Constitution. At the same time, the French Constitution of 1791 contained far more indigenous features. Chief among them were a unicameral legislature, the absence of genuine checks and balances, and an executive veto that was only suspensive.[31]

The Federal Constitution, just going into effect in 1789, might have had an even greater effect had it been better known in France. As it is, certain current French scholars argue it could not possibly have had much influence upon the Constitution of 1791.[32] Even after it became better known, they contend, the Federal Constitution exercised minimal influence upon the French constitutions framed later in the 1790s decade.[33]

In Poland the abortive Polish Constitution of 1791 reflected a bold attempt by reformers to reorganize the government in the spirit of the Federal Constitution. Although this Polish Constitution was never put into practice, it represented an effort to do away with the old custom of electing the king by the nobles which reputedly had torn the country apart. Once again the American example did not quite fit Poland's needs. The reformers, who were more or less democratic, nevertheless called for a stronger executive—something only a hereditary king could offer. Paradoxically, the Polish nobles—the more conservative aristocrats and their followers—defended the idea of an elected executive, or elected king; it was they who pointed to America's revolutionary experience to support their case.[34]

What has not been sufficiently appreciated by contemporary scholars to date is the degree to which the Federal Constitution influenced England at the time. Indeed, the Federal Constitution led some English radicals to change their views about the British Constitution. One scholar made an extensive review of the writings of forty-five of the most important English republicans active during the last quarter of the eighteenth century. He argued that their conception of the British Constitution was transformed as a result of their study of the American Revolution and its aftermath. "Specifically, the ideas of constitutionalism, republicanism, and popular sovereignty," he concluded, "were defined in a more democratic way in order to bring English republican theory in line with what appeared to be American practice."[35] The ramifications of these important findings remain as yet unexplored, but they reveal the indirect way in which the Federal Constitution exercised a powerful and important influence on the former mother country.

In Sweden the Federal Constitution served a different function—that of a precipitant of revolution. When the Federal Constitution was framed in America, it was immediately published in translation in Sweden. Influenced by such American ideas, Swedish nobles began to consider a coup against their absolute monarch. When in 1809 the revolution was finally achieved, some nobles wanted to establish a congress patterned after that of the United States. Strong class interests prevailed, however, and the old Riksdag of four estates was reconstituted.[36]

The reformist elements in Russia which resulted in the Decembrist movement were also influenced by the American document in a somewhat similar way. Many Decembrists came from the highest aristocracy. They had served as officers in the Russian armies, battled against Napoleon in 1812, and occupied Paris in 1815. Traveling across Europe as conquerors, they were exposed to liberal ideas, including those of France and indirectly those of America. Soon these more liberal nobles organized themselves into secret societies to achieve two goals: the abolition of serfdom and the establishment of representative government to restrict autocratic power. A few extremists even hoped for a republic. Significantly enough, both the more "radical" Decembrists like Pavel Ivanovich Pestel who advocated a republic, and Nikita Murav'ev who favored a limited monarchy were influenced by American constitutionalism. Murav'ev's draft for a constitution—providing for a constitutional monarchy and a federal organization of the Russian empire—clearly followed the pattern of the Federal Constitution. The Decembrist conspiracy which came to a head in 1825, however, was ruthlessly crushed. Many of its ideas survived, nevertheless, in the writings of Alexander Herzen, the liberal socialist, and others.[37]

One indirect way the Federal Constitution affected Europe was through its influence upon the Belgian Constitution of 1831, a constitution that provided the prototype for European constitutional monarchies for a full century after it was framed.[38] The Belgian document was one of the most eclectic constitutions ever framed in Europe. Delegates made use of French, British, and American ideas as well as drawing upon earlier Belgian constitutions. In fact, more than one-third of the document was derived from the French Constitution of 1830 alone.[39] From the United States the Belgians borrowed a bill of rights as sweeping as that found in the first state constitutions and the Federal Constitution. The Belgians also introduced another innovation to European constitutionalism—the principle of separation of church and state—one of the most radical features of the Federal Constitution. The Belgian Constitution emerged as one of the most liberal on the continent, permitting freedom of religion, assembly, and the press. Through the agency of the Belgian Constitution, which was imitated extensively throughout Europe, many features of American constitutionalism were indirectly brought to other European countries. At the same time, however, the

Belgians established a constitutional monarchy rather than a republic and differed in that important respect from the American constitutional system.

The European revolutions of 1848 represented the second major wave of American constitutional influence. A series of uprisings against established authority swept across the continent—in France, in the major states of Germany, within the Hapsburg Empire, and in northern and central Italy. Although these revolutions were crushed, their impact upon the political development of Europe was nevertheless profound. The upheavals produced important changes, many of them constitutional in character, and European revolutionaries at times looked to the Federal Constitution as a model.

In Germany, copies of the Declaration of Independence and the Federal Constitution once again became available and were widely circulated. Members of the Frankfurt Assembly in 1848–49 prepared a federal and liberal constitution. Although this ill-fated constitution was never implemented, assembly members wrote an eloquent statement on the rights of the individual, equality before the law, and parliamentary representation. In their deliberations they constantly discussed the Federal Constitution. They borrowed freely from it both in broad matters of principle and in details of practice while drafting their own document. Time and again they defended an article by declaring that it resembled an American example. One deputy argued that the "instructive example of America . . . had been the model of the preparatory commission, and one could not, without damage, deviate from it."[40]

Many parts of the Frankfurt Constitution bore a distinct American imprint. The German monarch's powers, for example, were consciously patterned after those of the American president. The Reichgericht was modelled somewhat on the United States Supreme Court. Two key articles were drawn almost word-for-word from the American Constitution: one conferred a virtual monopoly over foreign relations upon the new German union, and the other provided for direct elections to the Reichstag.[41]

The Frankfurt Constitution also made it easier for the Germans to entertain the idea of judicial review—the one American constitutional feature all but neglected in Europe at this time. One member of the Frankfurt Assembly urged the establishment of a supreme court with powers of judicial review. Others voiced opposition, fearing the princes in the German states would take advantage of judicial review to defend their monarchical status. The proponents for judicial review pressed hard for their position. One of them, Professor Mittermaier of Heidelberg offered this peroration: "What is considered the finest ornament of the American constitution?" The Supreme Court, he answered. "The

[American] Constitution," he declared, "owes its life, its strength, the certainty of its provisions in detail to the Supreme Court." "Let us follow the example of the United States," he added, "and we'll earn the most marvellous fruit. Give us this keystone for our constitution." The Germans already had had experience with a form of constitutional review, but America's example made it easier for the Frankfurt Assembly to accept the idea of judicial review. The Frankfurt constitution was stillborn, however, and Germans had to wait until the Weimar Republic of 1919 to make a start toward judicial guardianship.[42]

In at least two other respects, American features either were misunderstood or functioned quite differently in Germany. The Frankfurt framers had the new German union guarantee the fundamental rights of its citizens against any inroads by the member states. They did so in the belief that they were imitating the Federal Bill of Rights, whereas the first ten amendments actually protected the American people from any intrusion upon civil liberties by the federal government. The German drafters thus failed to introduce the American version of a bill of rights despite their intention to do so. The American version of federalism, moreover, was to operate quite differently in the Frankfurt Constitution. Its effects, however, resonated down through the years and affected Germany in later constitutions.[43]

The French Constitution of 1848 also was influenced by America's Federal Constitution. Certain of its features closely resembled the American model, and one of its major authors was none other than Alexis de Tocqueville. But there is a historiographical dispute regarding the extent of the American influence. One exhaustive study of the evolution of French constitutionalism mentions America only twice.[44] Another scholar, however, concluded that parts of the document were clearly inspired by the American model because of certain important features the two had in common: the direct popular election of the president, the requirement that a candidate be a native-born Frenchman, the provision for a vice president—though he was to be designated by the assembly for an interim period, the appointment by the president of ministers who would be responsible to him and not to the legislature, and the absence of any power of dissolution on the part of the president.[45]

In several important respects, however, the French Constitution of 1848 quite obviously diverged from its American counterpart. The most significant difference was the absence of checks and balances. The French also avoided both the federalism and bicameralism of the Federal Constitution because they did not wish sovereignty to be divided. Finally, one commentator observed that the French republicans of 1848 were "generally in agreement that the fate of the poor classes must become a major preoccupation of the state."[46] In any case, the French Constitution of 1848 proved short-lived; it soon gave way to a document that had far less in common with the Federal Constitution.

The Swiss Constitution of 1848, on the other hand, consciously and deliberately emulated the Federal Constitution. In two important respects American influence proved to be long-lasting in Swiss constitutional history: the adaptation of the American version of federalism to Switzerland's specific situation and the adoption of the bicameral form of government. The two countries had much in common and consequently could consider much the same constitutional solutions. Both were republics; both had grown into a federal union under somewhat similar circumstances; and both had to reconcile the demands of a heterogeneous population. The framers of the Swiss Constitution in 1848 and America's founding fathers in 1787 also faced a similar problem: how to form a well-balanced union out of a loose confederacy of cantons or states that were altogether too sovereign and very unequal in terms of territory and population.

Looking closely at the experience of the United States, the Swiss framers accepted an adaptation of the American style of federalism when it came to reconciling state sovereignty and federal power. They created a strong federal state in which the powers of the central and cantonal governments were set down with extreme precision. The express powers of the central government were enunciated in such great detail, however, as to leave little room for any doctrine of implied powers. All residual powers not expressly granted to the federal government remained in the hands of the cantonal authorities—though in many respects the Swiss central government had much wider authority than did that of the United States.

At the same time, the Swiss federal government had a two-house legislature similar to that of the United States. For the first time—with only one exception—the idea of a single legislative body in Switzerland was dropped. The Council of States resembling the American Senate was set up, though it never acquired the position of authority of its American counterpart. Nor for that matter was the division of power between the various branches of the federal government as precisely drawn as in the United States. The relations between the legislative and executive branches, moreover, differed sharply from the American system.[47] Despite some obvious and important differences, the two leading authorities on Swiss constitutional history—one a Swiss and the other an American—concluded that the Swiss Constitution of 1848 presented a close analogy to the Federal Constitution of 1787.[48]

The influence of the Federal Constitution in Germany, France, and Switzerland reveals that the revolutions of 1848 were strongly affected by the American constitutional precedents. Whenever Europeans experienced revolutions on a large scale—as in the case of the French

Revolution and its aftermath or the upheavals of 1848—they invariably turned to constitutional reform. And wherever constitutional reforms were in the air, the American Constitution was often sought out as a model to be debated, discussed, and, in some instances, adapted to a country's needs.

THE *FEDERALIST PAPERS*

The *Federalist Papers*, generally acknowledged as the classic American study on government, exercised considerable influence not only within the United States but in Europe from the time of their publication in the 1780s to 1848. European constitution-makers read and cited these essays for many reasons: their analysis of the nature of republican government, their comments on the American version of federalism, and their exposition of the bicameral system. Charles A. Beard's conclusion that the essays represented "the most instructive work on political science ever written in the United States" may be justified, given the use to which the *Federalist Papers* were put in Europe.[49]

The *Federalist Papers* had their most immediate influence abroad in France. Shortly after their publication in America, the essays were being quoted in the French National Assembly debates. In the main they were cited in debates concerning the concept of federalism as it might be applied in France.[50] The second and third editions of the complete work appeared for the first time in Paris in 1792. During the summer of that same year, the assembly conferred honorary membership upon Hamilton and Madison for "their writing." Such official recognition shows how important and relevant the essays were to the French.[51]

The *Federalist Papers* fell in and out of favor in subsequent French history. In 1793 when the concept of federalism came under suspicion in France, the essays were in temporary disrepute. That gifted French observer of American affairs, Tocqueville, later lauded the work in 1835 in his classic study *Democracy in America*: "I shall often have occasion to quote *The Federalist* in this work. . . . [It] is an excellent book, which ought to be familiar to the statesmen of all countries."[52] Indeed, Tocqueville was to play an important role in spreading the ideas of the American work throughout Europe.[53]

In Germany the *Federalist Papers* exercised less influence at first because the German states were still striving for unification. As late as the end of the eighteenth century, the American version of federalism was little in evidence.[54] But interest in America increased in the 1820s and 1830s, especially after Tocqueville's work appeared in two German translations in 1836. It was, however, Robert von Mohl, "Germany's Tocqueville," who set the agenda for the discussion of constitutional issues in that country for three decades. In 1824 when he published his first book on

America, Mohl drew frequently upon the *Federalist Papers*. Regarded as one of Germany's greatest political scientists, Mohl started on his work when he realized that a systematic study of the American Constitution had yet to be done. His book was based mainly on the text of the Federal Constitution, the debates in the Philadelphia Convention, the *Federalist Papers*, and other key documents.[55]

The essays continued to play an increasingly important role in Germany. At the Frankfurt Assembly in 1848, the constitutional committee made use of Mohl's work. Moreover, there is reason to believe that committee members referred specifically to the *Federalist Papers* when discussing the American version of federalism.[56] The essays occupied the attention of Mohl even more in his treatise on American government published in 1855. He praised the *Federalist Papers* as one of the best works published in the general field of politics and public law and among the most famous and useful theoretical studies on states' rights. "It would be difficult," he wrote, "to render a more careful and more brilliant account of the principles and the essential institutions of the American Constitution."[57] Two years earlier, Georg Waitz, a noted political theorist, elaborated on the principle of divided sovereignty—a doctrine discussed in the *Federalist Papers* and one which spread throughout Europe in part through Tocqueville's writings. Waitz's doctrine of divided sovereignty, derived from the American essays, was for decades the one generally accepted by German scholars discussing constitutional matters.[58]

In Switzerland two of the most prominent advocates of the American system of government during the 1830s—Ignaz P. V. Troxler and James Fazy—were deeply influenced by the *Federalist Papers*.[59] Troxler, perhaps more than any other single person, was responsible for the adoption of the American bicameral system in Switzerland. Fazy looked upon the bicameral system as the most valuable feature of the Federal Constitution. When he was in political control in Geneva in 1847, he expressly instructed the delegates in the Diet to vote in favor of such a system.[60]

The *Federalist Papers*, however, were to have their greatest effect in Europe after the 1848 upheavals. This was particularly true when the American style of federalism gained favor among constitution-makers and intellectuals in France, Germany, Italy, and in the British empire later in the nineteenth century. In the twentieth century, moreover, the essays were generally recognized as having some bearing not only on problems of constitutional government and federalism within particular nations but for their importance for international federal movements as well. Charles A. Beard, among others, recommended the *Federalist Papers* be studied because the federalism they proposed when applied on an international level carried with it a promise for lasting world peace.[61]

THE FEDERAL BILL OF RIGHTS

The Federal Bill of Rights, adopted as the first ten amendments to the Constitution, is the final founding text to be discussed. Their adoption in 1791 represented a fitting climax to the great age of constitution-making that had commenced in America in 1776. The Federal Bill of Rights constituted the culmination of the idea of law as a check on governmental power.

From an international perspective, the bill of rights tradition has a complicated and complex past. The idea that a human being could possess certain unalienable rights stretches back to antiquity, the medieval period, and the Renaissance. In more modern times, the rights set forth in the English documents mentioned previously found their way to the American colonies. The Declaration of Independence, first state constitutions, and Federal Bill of Rights, in fact, not only reflected many of the ideas in these English documents but in some instances repeated the same language. French philosophers of the Enlightenment writing about the doctrine of rights also exercised a powerful influence upon the thinking of America's founding fathers. But in the main, the Federal Bill of Rights was patterned in large part after the antecedents established in the American state bills of rights, which actually had put the idea into practice for the first time. Unlike the state bills of rights, however, the ten amendments protected individual rights from the actions of the federal government and set yet another pattern for other nations to follow.

The French Declaration of the Rights of Man and the Citizen of 1789, likewise issued on the national level, was influenced by the American state bills of rights, as noted previously. Certainly the French followed the same procedure: they too listed rights, set them down in a numbered series, and then attached them as a document distinct from the constitution.[62] The French Declaration itself was later incorporated into the French Constitution of 1791, and there were similar declarations in the French Constitutions of 1793 and 1795.

This combined Anglo-American-French tradition clearly established a precedent in Europe when French armies advanced through Europe in the 1790s. Between 1796 and 1799, ten constitutions were written for sister republics stretching from Holland to Italy. All the constitutions of these revolutionary regimes began with declarations of rights.[63]

Following the French Revolution, Belgium was the next country to adopt a bill of rights. The Belgian Constitution of 1831 incorporated a declaration similar in many particulars to the French Declaration of 1789 and the Federal Bill of Rights. But the Belgian Constitution approached the protection of rights from a practical point of view that resembled somewhat more the American model: it forbade acts that interfered with the exercise of these rights.[64]

During the revolutions of 1848, two countries seriously discussed a declaration of rights. In the ill-fated Frankfurt Constitution, the framers, as noted, adopted a declaration of the fundamental rights of the German people in the mistaken belief that they were imitating the Federal Bill of Rights. In Italy the Piedmont Constitution of 1848 contained a declaration of the rights of citizens which followed the model of the Belgian Constitution. In this respect, therefore, the Piedmont Constitution might be considered as showing an indirect American influence.[65]

But it was after 1848 in Europe—in Germany in 1919, Bavaria in 1919, Austria and Czechoslovakia in 1920, Greece in 1927, and Lithuania in 1928—that the Anglo-American-French bill of rights tradition best served as a model. Indeed, the example set by England, the United States, and France was followed not only in Europe but throughout Latin America, Asia, and Africa in the course of the nineteenth and twentieth centuries.

CONCLUSION

The conclusion that American constitutionalism affected Europe between the years 1776 and 1848 is indisputable. Having made the argument for American constitutional influence, however, it is necessary to keep in mind certain qualifications. It should be reemphasized that most of Europe's constitutions during this period were influenced far more by indigenous practices and by European constitutional traditions. European constitution-makers looked more to France than to the United States for their models and guidance. There were, in addition, other European constitutional traditions that served as guides, notably the parliamentary constitutionalism of Britain, the Spanish Constitution of 1812, and the seminal Belgian Constitution of 1831. It should also be remembered that the idea of republicanism, of which America provided a living example, was not generally favored: before the revolutions of 1848 republicanism was considered a greater danger to the established order than socialism, and the forces of liberalism in general were weak. These qualifications, however, do not negate the thesis that American constitutionalism had a significant influence in Europe during "the age of the democratic revolution."

What happened after 1848 to bring to a close this era of influence of American constitutionalism in Europe? Briefly put, the 1776–1848 period marked an age when many American and European constitution-makers and writers dreamed of constitutional formulations along more universal lines as a result of the ideas of the European Enlightenment and the American and French revolutions. Constitutional formulations after 1848, however, went off in different directions for at least three reasons.

With the rise of the German historical school of legal thought led by

Friedrich Karl von Savigny, whose great works appeared in the early 1800s, the notion spread that the constitutions and legal institutions of a people were an indigenous expression of their culture and could not be externally imposed. German jurists, like Savigny, were opposed to the natural law theories incorporated in the French and American constitutions, which implied that more universal constitutional formulations were possible. Constitution-makers and legal theorists the world over, as a result, began to think along different lines.

A second development that blunted the influence of American constitutionalism was the rise of a competing ideology—socialism. As far back as the French Constitution of 1791, there was great concern shown for the social rights of the poor and dependent classes. With the publication of the *Communist Manifesto* in 1848, a new universalism was born which addressed these social questions more directly in constitutional terms. The universalism of the socialist model—with its greater emphasis on economic justice and more equitable distribution of property—contrasted sharply with the universalism implied in the American model, which stressed more the civil liberties of citizens and rights of private property. Faced with an alternative model in the midst of the Industrial Revolution, many Europeans turned more to socialist constitutional formulations in the late nineteenth century.

The post–1848 period saw the rise of a third development that made American constitutionalism less attractive to the peoples of Europe: the renewed emphasis on nationalism. Nationalism, as an ideology, flew in the face of any attempts at universal constitutional formulations. As early as the revolt in Naples in 1799 and the uprising of Spanish guerrillas in 1808, there were stirrings of cultural nationalism among many peoples—the Germans, Italians, Poles, Hungarians, and others. The nationalist movements that flowered in the revolutions of 1848 were obviously at odds with the universalism implicit in American constitutionalism.

The years after 1848 marked a temporary decline in the influence of American constitutionalism in Europe. Although it was to revive in the post–World War I and World War II periods, its highest peak, perhaps, had been reached in the era from 1776 to 1848. The reverberations of American constitutionalism experienced during this period were destined to influence not only Europe but the rest of the world down to the present day.

NOTES

Eight friends and colleagues were generous in helping to formulate many of the ideas expressed in this essay. The author acknowledges to them his deep gratitude: Peter Onuf, University of Virginia; Ronald Petrin, Oklahoma State University; Robert Kolesar, John Carroll University; Paul Lucas, Clark University; Francis Couvares, Amherst College; Milton Klein, Professor Emeritus, University of Tennessee; Walter F. Murphy, Princeton University; and Gerald Grob, Rutgers University.

1. Leonard Levy et al., *The Encyclopedia of the American Constitution*, 4 vols. (New York: Macmillan Company, 1986), 2:473, stresses that American historians tend to use the term "constitutionalism" as a shorthand reference to the constitutional thought of the founding period.

2. Robert R. Palmer, *The Age of The Democratic Revolution*, 2 vols. (Princeton, N.J.: Princeton University Press, 1959–64).

3. Peter Gay, *The Enlightenment*, 2 vols. (New York: Knopf, 1966 and 1969), 2:558–60.

4. See Bernard Bailyn, *Ideological Origins of the American Revolution* (Cambridge, Mass.: Harvard University Press, 1967); and Gordon S. Wood, *Creation of the American Republic, 1776–1787* (Chapel Hill: University of North Carolina Press, 1969). Bailyn and Wood deemphasized Locke's influence as a formal thinker and emphasized instead informal writers and pamphleteers like John Trenchard and Thomas Gordon. But Locke is making a comeback. See Thomas Pangle, *Spirit of Modern Republicanism* (Chicago: University of Chicago Press, 1988); John Murrin, "Can Liberals Be Patriots?" in Robert P. Davidow, ed. *Natural Rights and Natural Law* (Fairfax, Va.: George Mason University Printing Press, 1986), 47 and 60; Jay Fliegelman, *Prodigals and Pilgrims* (New York: Cambridge University Press, 1982); and Donald S. Lutz, *Origins of American Constitutionalism* (Baton Rouge: Louisiana State University Press, 1988). For support of the idea that few colonists had actually read Locke's famous *Two Treatises of Government*, see Oscar Handlin and Lilian Handlin, "Who Read Locke? Words and Acts in the Revolution," *American Scholar* (1989): 545–56.

5. Robert R. Palmer, "The Impact of the American Revolution Abroad," Library of Congress Symposia on the American Revolution, *The Impact of the American Revolution Abroad* (Washington, D.C.: Library of Congress, 1976), 13.

6. Carl Becker, "Declaration of Independence," *Encyclopedia of the Social Sciences* (New York, 1931), 5:47.

7. Thad W. Tate, "The Social Contract in America, 1774–1787: Revolutionary Theory as a Conservative Instrument," *William and Mary Quarterly*, 3d series, 22 (1965): 375–91.

8. David M. Ellis et al., *A History of New York State* (Ithaca, N.Y.: Cornell University Press), 113.

9. Benjamin F. Wright, *Consensus and Continuity: 1776–1787* (Boston, Mass.: Boston University Press, 1958), 8–9.

10. Ibid. 20; and Palmer, "The Impact of the American Revolution Abroad," 13.

11. John Hawgood, *Modern Constitutions Since 1787* (New York: Van Nostrand, 1939), 2–3.

12. Palmer, *The Age of the Democratic Revolution*, 1:262.

13. Crane Brinton, *Decade of Revolution, 1789–1799* (New York: Harper and Brothers, 1934), 120; and Geoffrey Brunn, *Europe and the French Imperium, 1799–1814* (New York: Harper and Brothers, 1938), 6.

14. Palmer, "Impact of the American Revolution Abroad," 12–13.

15. Joyce Appleby, "The Jefferson-Adams Rupture and the First French Translation of John Adams' *Defence*," *American Historical Review* 73 (1968): 1084–

91, especially 1089; and Henry E. Bourne, "American Constitutional Precedents in the French National Assembly," *American Historical Review* 8 (1902–3): 466–90.

16. The literature on this controversy is voluminous and stretches back to the discussion between Georg Jellinek and Émile Doumergue around the early 1900s. For a more complete discussion of the historiography on this subject, see the bibliographical essay.

17. Palmer, "Impact of the American Revolution Abroad," 14. All the derivative constitutions and most of the satellite states from the French Revolution were short-lived. Grand Duke Leopold of Tuscany worked out a project from 1779 to 1782 for a constitution based on the Virginia Constitution of 1776 as well. See Palmer, *The Age of the Democratic Revolution*, 1:385–86.

18. Thomas K. Gorman, *America and Belgium* (London: T. F. Unwin, 1925), vii; and Palmer, *The Age of the Democratic Revolution*, 1:353.

19. Jan Willem Schulte Nordholt, "The Impact of the American Revolution on the Dutch Republic," Library of Congress Symposia on the American Revolution, *Impact of the American Revolution Abroad*, 52; and Simon Schama, *Patriots and Liberators* (New York: Knopf, 1977), 61.

20. Schama, *Patriots and Liberators*, 95.

21. Jan Willem Schulte Nordholt, *The Dutch Republic and American Independence* (Chapel Hill: University of N.C. Press, 1982), 270–71.

22. Franklin Scott, *The United States and Scandinavia* (Cambridge, Mass.: Harvard University Press, 1950), 65–66; Richard B. Morris, *Emerging Nations and the American Revolution* (New York: Harper & Row, 1970), 95–96; and Hawgood, *Modern Constitutions Since 1787*, 54–58.

23. Thomas Jefferson to A. Coray [Adamantias Korais], Oct. 31, 1823, Andrew A. Lipscomb, ed. *Writings of Thomas Jefferson*, 20 vols. (Washington, D.C.: Thomas Jefferson Memorial Association, 1903), 15:480–94; Harris Booras, *Hellenic Independence and America's Contribution to the Cause* (Rutland, Vt.: Tuttle, 1948), 60 and 159; and Stephen Larrabee, *Hellas Observed* (New York: New York University Press, 1957), 34.

24. Alexander N. Radishchev, *A Journey from St. Petersburg to Moscow* (Cambridge, Mass.: Harvard University Press, 1958), 184–86.

25. Merrill Jensen, *The Articles of Confederation* (Madison: University of Wisconsin Press, 1962) and *The New Nation* (New York: Knopf, 1950).

26. Carl J. Friedrich, *Impact of American Constitutionalism Abroad* (Boston, Mass.: Boston University Press, 1967), 45.

27. Durand Echeverria, "French Publications of the Declaration of Independence and the American Constitutions," *Papers of the Bibliographical Society of America* 47 (1953): 323.

28. Ernst H. Kossman, *The Low Countries, 1780–1940* (Oxford: Clarendon Press, 1978), 60; and Palmer, "Impact of the American Revolution Abroad," 15.

29. Schulte Nordholt, *The Dutch Republic and American Independence*, 11–12, 265–66.

30. Bourne, "American Constitutional Precedents in the French National Assembly," 471–86; and Palmer, *The Age of the Democratic Revolution*, 1:489–502. According to Michel Debré, French constitutional theorists have tended to view the separation of powers doctrine through the eyes of Carre de Malberg, who questioned whether Montesquieu's concept—which envisaged a dual role of a chief of state and distinct domains for the executive and legislative branches,

each limiting the power of the other—ever applied to French *republican* regimes. See Nicholas Wahl, "Aux origines de la nouvelle constitution," *Revue francaise de science politique* 9, no. 1 (1959): 58.

31. Guy Richard, *Les institutions politiques de la France de Louis XV á Giscard d'Estaing* (Paris: Flammarion, 1979), 131–48.

32. Jacques Godechot, "L'Influence des États-Unis sur les Constitutions Francaises de l'Époque Revolutionaire (1789–1799)," unpublished paper, 26. This paper was graciously shared by Professor Albert P. Blaustein of Rutgers University.

33. Ibid., 35 and 42. For an attempt by one French deputy in 1793 to propose a veto power copied from the American Constitution, see Maurice J. C. Vile, *Constitutionalism and the Separation of Powers* (Oxford: Clarendon Press, 1967), 196.

34. Manfred Kridl et al., *For Your Freedom and Ours* (New York: Frederick Ungar, 1943), 66–67; and Palmer, "Impact of the American Revolution Abroad," 15.

35. Arthur Sheps, "The American Revolution and the Transformation of English Republicanism," *Historical Reflections* 2 (1975): 3–28.

36. Halvdan Koht, *American Spirit in Europe* (New York: Atheneum, 1968), 21.

37. David Hecht, ed., *Russian Radicals Look to America, 1825–1894* (Cambridge, Mass.: Harvard University Press, 1947), 17–19; and Marc Raeff, ed., *The Decembrist Movement* (Englewood Cliffs, N.J.: Prentice-Hall, 1966), 100–118.

38. Hawgood, *Modern Constitutions since 1787*, 146.

39. Kossman, *The Low Countries, 1780–1940*, 157.

40. Professor Mittermaier quoted in Friedrich, *Impact of American Constitutionalism Abroad*, 26; and Robert C. Binkley, "The Holy Roman Empire Versus the United States: Patterns for Constitution-Making in Central Europe," in Conyers Read, ed., *The Constitution Reconsidered*, rev. ed. (New York: Harper & Row, 1968), 278. The key work is Eckhart G. Franz, *Das Amerikabild der deutschen Revolution von 1848* (Heidelberg: C. Winter, 1958).

41. Ibid.

42. Friedrich, *Impact of American Constitutionalism Abroad*, 81–82.

43. Binkley, "The Holy Roman Empire versus the United States: Patterns for Constitution-Making in Central Europe," 278–79.

44. Maurice Deslandres, *Histoire constitutionnelle de la France de 1789 à 1870*, 3 vols. (Paris: Armand Colin and Sirey, 1932) 2:344–92.

45. Andre Hauriou and Jean Gicquel, *Droit constitutionnel et institutions politiques*, 7th ed. (Paris: Editiones Montchrestien, 1980), 813–14.

46. Jean Petot, *Les grandes étapes du régime républican français, 1792–1969: Études d'histoire politique et constitutionnelle* (Paris: Cujas, 1970), 276–77; for the fullest treatment, see Eugene N. Curtis, "The French Assembly of 1848 and American Constitutional Doctrines," Ph.D. diss., Columbia University, 1917.

47. Hawgood, *Modern Constitutions Since 1787*, 184.

48. William E. Rappard, "Pennsylvania and Switzerland: The American Origins of the Swiss Constitution," in *Studies in Political Science and Sociology* (Philadelphia, Penn., 1941), 49–121; William E. Rappard, *La Constitution Fédérale de la Suisse* (Neuchatel, Switzerland, 1948); and Myron L. Tripp, *The Swiss and*

United States Federal Constitutional Systems: A Comparative Study (Paris: Librairie Sociale et Economique, 1940). Despite the obvious analogies between the American Constitution and the Swiss Constitution of 1848, there were great differences between the two documents as well as in the historical situations. Much of the Swiss Constitution was derivative and relied upon other foreign influences as well as indigenous needs. The executive branch in the Swiss system (a federal council) differed sharply from the executive in the United States, where a single executive is completely separate under the separation of powers. Moreover, the division of powers between the different branches of the federal government in Switzerland differed from that in the United States. There was also no attempt to imitate the United States Supreme Court. The federal government was given greater power to intervene in cantonal matters than was the case in the United States into state affairs.

49. Charles A. Beard, ed., *The Enduring Federalist* (New York: Doubleday, 1948), 10.

50. Godechot, "L'Influence des États-Unis sur les Constitutions Françaises de l'Époque Revolutionaire (1789–1799)," 38–39.

51. Gottfried Dietze, *The Federalist* (Baltimore, Md.: Johns Hopkins University Press, 1960), 10.

52. Ibid., 11.

53. Ibid., 13.

54. Horst Dippel, *Germany and the American Revolution* (Chapel Hill: University of North Carolina Press, 1977), 174.

55. Gottfried Dietze, "Robert von Mohl, Germany's de Tocqueville," in Gottfried Dietze, ed., *Essays on the American Constitution* (Englewood Cliffs, N.J.: Prentice-Hall, 1964), 188–92.

56. Dietze, *The Federalist*, 12.

57. Quoted in Dietze, *The Federalist*, 13.

58. Ibid.

59. George Sauser-Hall, *Political Institutions of Switzerland* (Zurich: Swiss Tourist Office Pub. Dept., 1946), 200.

60. Rappard, "Pennsylvania and Switzerland: The American Origins of the Swiss Constitution," 91 and 104.

61. Dietze, *The Federalist*, 16–17; and Roy P. Fairfield, ed., *Federalist Papers* (New York: Anchor Books, 1961), especially the bibliographical appendix.

62. Palmer, *The Age of the Democratic Revolution*, 1:521.

63. Ibid., 2:487.

64. Hawgood, *Modern Constitutions Since 1787*, 142.

65. Ibid., 171–72.

2

North American Constitutionalism and Spanish America:

"A SPECIAL LOCK ORDERED BY CATALOGUE, WHICH ARRIVED WITH THE WRONG INSTRUCTIONS AND NO KEYS"?

Robert J. Kolesar

Robert Kolesar finds that North American constitutionalism, European Enlightenment ideas, and historic strands of the Hispanic constitutional tradition all contributed to the formulation of Latin American constitutionalism. Although Kolesar observes that many of the documents, procedures, and institutions associated with North American constitutionalism became models for Latin American constitution-makers or influenced them in other ways, he concludes that the imitation that took place was not a case of straightforward borrowing. Time and again, when Latin Americans found that North American constitutional ideals, ideas, and institutions failed to fit their indigenous conditions, they modified them accordingly. Thus, while the North American constitutional tradition influenced Latin American nations, its reception differed from country to country, and it was shaped to conform to long-lasting colonial traditions, unique circumstances, and enduring local conflicts.

In Isabel Allende's *House of the Spirits*, the most recent of an impressive number of contemporary Latin American novels which search the historical experience of Hispanic American culture, the patriarch of the Trueba family presides over two worlds. In one, he lives in a city mansion of "German stained glass windows, moldings carved in Austria, faucets of English bronze, Italian marble floors, and special locks ordered by catalogue from the United States, which arrived with the wrong instructions and no keys." It is a world far removed from that of his rural estate of Hispanic traditions.

The contradictions between those worlds is one of the central themes of the historical experience of Latin America. The significance of the frequent borrowings from constitutional documents of the United States contained in Latin American constitutions has often been discounted on the basis that constitutional principles have had little impact on the actual practices of Latin American politics. In this view, North American constitutional principles have been "special locks ordered by catalogue from the United States, which arrived with the wrong instructions and no keys," and failed to function because of their differences from Hispanic traditions.[1]

It is the premise of this essay that any consideration of the influence of North American constitutionalism on nineteenth-century Spanish America shows it to have been a far more complicated process than simple imitation. A number of questions need to be addressed. Why did Spanish Americans often use North American constitutionalism as a model? How were the constitutional documents of the United States disseminated in Spanish America? How did the influence of North American constitutionalism operate in specific political contexts? And what role have constitutional principles served in Latin American political culture? It is hoped that consideration of these questions will help to establish general propositions that must be addressed when assessing the influence of North American constitutionalism abroad.

I

Although North American constitutional documents were often used as models by Spanish Americans, it is a mistake to view that use removed from either the political realities of Latin America or the general current of Western ideas. Faced with the problems of reconstructing authority and controlling the political influence of the Catholic Church and the military in newly independent nations, Spanish Americans looked to a number of political models, including those of their own Spanish traditions as well as those from Britain, France, and the United States. Fully acquainted with the European sources of Enlightenment philosophies, they viewed the constitutional documents of the United States within that context. The principles of the Enlightenment were essential to the development of nineteenth-century Spanish American liberalism. As John Lynch has noted, those principles were "brought into political focus" by both the American and French Revolutions. And Spanish Americans were notoriously eclectic in forging political theories: to them, North American constitutionalism was one practical, workable embodiment of Enlightenment political theories.[2]

Thus, to Spanish Americans, North American constitutional ideas were not unique, nor did they necessarily oppose or contradict the influence of other constitutional varieties based on Enlightenment principles. In Mexico and Chile, for example, the influence of North American constitutionalism was complementary with that of the liberal Spanish Constitution of 1812. The appeal of the United States was heightened, however, by the anti-Spanish and anti-European tenor of the independence movement and a sentiment of solidarity with the ex-colonies of North America. And the appeal of the French Revolution as a political model was lessened dramatically by the slave revolt in the French colony of Saint-Domingue in 1791, as well as by the course of revolutionary events in France itself. In 1799, for example, Venezuela's Francisco de Miranda observed that "We have before us two great examples, the American and the French Revolutions. Let us prudently imitate the first and carefully shun the second."[3]

But most importantly, the influence of North American constitutionalism, and specific instances of the use of constitutional documents of the United States, was closely associated with federalism. The first Spanish American republican constitution—the Venezuelan of 1811—was closely patterned on that of the United States, consciously drawing its federal structure from the model that "had been well proved by the experience of the United States."[4] And it is on the basis of federal structure that Latin American constitutions have been criticized most often: for reflecting borrowed ideology rather than Latin American traditions, for dividing previously unified nations rather than uniting divided nations, and for masking the continued centralization of power.[5] Certainly the banners "federalist" and "centralist" have at times been no more than the labels of personalist factions in Latin American history. But it does not follow from that observation that Latin American federalism has had no substantive meaning.

The use of federal constitutional structures in nineteenth-century Spanish America reflected and responded to a number of conditions within the area's own historical experience and political traditions. Among the elements contributing to the emergence of Latin American federalism and the use of constitutional precedents drawn from the experience of the United States were several features: historic strands of municipal and regional autonomy within the Hispanic political tradition, more recent administrative divisions within the centralized Spanish empire, and divergent regional economic and social interests in the emerging nations of nineteenth-century Spanish America.[6]

Throughout Spanish America, federalism was used by regional social and economic groups in their efforts to try to break the political and economic monopolies of the capital cities. The displacement of colonial power touched off struggles between outlying provinces and the metropolitan centers of economic and political power as well as competition between striving but socially peripheral elites and those entrenched in the administrative and economic centers. Venezuela, for example, had existed as a political unit only since 1777. Regional social, ethnic, and economic differences contributed to strong particularist sentiment against the capital, Caracas. In Chile, the North American example was cited by provincial representatives in their struggle for equal representation with Chile's capital city. Before the adoption of the Mexican Federal Constitution of 1824, the Mexican provinces had become virtually independent. And in Uruguay, José Artigas looked to North American constitutionalism for a model of provincial authority in his struggle against the hegemony of Buenos Aires—a struggle linked to the economic interests of Uruguay in free trade.[7] It is quite clear that regionalism was an intensely strong force in nineteenth-century Spanish American political development. Federalism was far from "foreign" to the Latin American historical experience: it was, in case after case, the banner of regional interests and often proved to be an important means of giving political unity to nations that shared little geographic, economic, or social coherence.

The social and economic success of the United States served as a third inducement to Spanish Americans to utilize North American constitutional principles. Many members of the revolutionary generation had a strong faith in the efficacy of constitutional and institutional reform: they believed that constitutions could remake their society. To many, independence from Spain was but the first step in liberating their nations from the crust of traditions and inherited privileges. Camilio Henríquez's *Aurora de Chile* proclaimed in its first edition that "there is no law, no custom that ought to remain fixed if from it proceeds a detriment, an inconvenience, a disturbance of the body politic." Throughout Spanish America, liberals who promoted social and economic progress pointed to the example of the United States: they attributed its success not to the characteristics of its people but to its political institutions. José Miguel Infante, the leader of the Chilean federalists, for example, told Chileans that "Washington did so much good for mankind because the LAWS OF THE NORTH AMERICAN FEDERATION placed him in the happy position of being unable to do bad."[8]

II

Spanish American use of North American constitutionalism was furthered also by direct North American proselytizing to some extent. The influence of North American constitutionalism was thus inextricably woven into relations between the Americas. Those relations were marked by deep-seated notions of racial and religious superiority held by the

North Americans. As early as 1699, the North American urge to convert the Spanish colonies was expressed by Cotton Mather's *Essay to convey religion into the Spanish Indies*. The long colonial economic and political rivalry of North Americans with Spain and its colonies further conditioned relations between the Americas. As Peggy Liss has shown, a complex mixture of religious mission and economic and political motives characterized North American contacts with the emerging Spanish American republics of the early nineteenth century. Ambivalent perceptions of each other held by North Americans and Spanish Americans also left their mark on the influence of North American constitutionalism in Spanish America.[9]

North American mariners carried constitutional documents to ports they called on in Spanish America well before the Spanish American wars of independence. Among the eighty North American ships that called on the far distant ports of Chile between 1788 and 1810 was the *Lelia Byrd*, which spent nine weeks in the port of Valparaiso in 1802. The owners, William Shaler and Richard Cleveland, spent their time in port discussing the advantages to the Chileans of throwing off their colonial yoke. "For the better promotion of the embryo cause," Cleveland and Shaler gave the Chileans a copy of the United States Constitution and a Spanish translation of the Declaration of Independence. After leaving Chile, Shaler continued his lectures in San Blas, Mexico. How many North American mariners consciously promoted North American political and constitutional ideas is unknown. It is also difficult to determine what immediate impact such propagandizing had. Certainly the efforts of Shaler and Cleveland did not play a causal role in the subsequent independence movement. But the documents that such men carried, as Simon Collier has noted in his study of the political ideas of Chilean independence, "were bound to play a part in any subsequent developments."[10]

Although North Americans played little active role in the Spanish American wars of independence, they did take interest in the constitutional development of the newly independent nations. They often offered aid and encouragement in the actual drafting of republican constitutions. In 1818, W. G. D. Worthington, United States Special Agent to Chile, authored and sent to the government of Chile a draft constitutional plan. In 1823, Stephen Austin did the same in Mexico. And in 1826, John M. Forbes, United States Charge d'Affaires in Buenos Aires, reported with an evident sense of satisfaction that a proposed constitution would "embrace most of the principles, and even the form of ours."[11]

The most active agent of the United States in Spanish America was Joel Roberts Poinsett, a Carolinian who hoped to extend North American institutions to all the nations of Spanish America. As the United States representative to Chile during the first period of de facto Chilean independence, the *patria vieja* of 1810–14, Poinsett offered to the patriot leadership a draft constitution closely patterned on that of the United States. A dozen years later in Mexico, Poinsett, as the United States Minister, took full advantage of his instructions. They called on him "to show on all occasions an unobstrusive readiness to explain the practical operation and the very great advantages which appertain to our system."[12]

Poinsett's influence was far from "unobstrusive" in either Chile or Mexico, however. As a result, the influence of the United States and the political principles it represented suffered a setback in both Chile and Mexico. In Chile, Poinsett became so involved with internal Chilean politics that he actually accompanied troops onto the battlefield. As the influence of the faction to which he had aligned himself declined in 1814, so did that of North American constitutional ideas. In Mexico, Poinsett again became intimately involved with one faction. His actions became so outrageous that in 1829 the Mexican government asked that he be recalled. The net result of Poinsett's meddling in Mexico's internal politics was to undercut previously favorable impressions Mexicans had had of North American political institutions.[13]

Interest in the United States in the establishment of republican governments in Spanish America, though real, was tempered by the exigencies of national interest as well as by a profound antipathy towards the institutions, race, and religion of Spanish Americans. Official policy was hesitant and somewhat ambivalent, constrained not only by desires to antagonize neither Spain nor Britain but also by Jefferson's embargo and the War of 1812. Moreover, Joel Poinsett's evident belief in the suitability of North American political institutions to Hispanic nations was not fully shared by his own countrymen. In 1806, John Adams likened plans for republican governments in Spanish America, then being promoted by Venezuela's Francisco de Miranda, to establishing democracies "among the birds, beasts, and fishes." Thomas Jefferson likewise had doubts about the fitness of Spanish Americans and wrote to Alexander von Humboldt that "History, I believe, furnishes no example of a priest-ridden people maintaining a free civil government."[14]

However much the North American revolutionary generation believed in the universality of the constitutional principles it had forged, that belief waned considerably by the middle of the nineteenth century. In part this was a consequence of a general hardening of North American racial attitudes—a situation which grew worse as a result of the war with Mexico. Conversely, North American racism made admiration of its institutions increasingly difficult for Latin Americans. As early as 1826 the newspaper *El Sol* of Mexico was clearly displeased by the "fanatical intolerance" of John Randolph's Senate speech in which he asserted that the United States should not associate as equals with the South Americans, who were descended from Africans. The ambivalent Mexican attitude of fear and admiration of the United States turned more hostile after the Texas revolution of 1836 and other acts of aggression.[15]

Spanish Americans played a much more important role in disseminating North American constitutional documents in the region than did North Americans themselves. As early as 1798, Spanish officials warned the home government of the printing of the United States Constitution by a Spanish American.[16] But it was not until the first years of the actual struggle for independence that North American documents became widely available.

On July 5, 1811, Venezuela became the first of the Spanish dominions to declare its independence. In that year the Venezuelan Manuel García de Sena published a volume of translations that included Thomas Paine's *Common Sense*, the American Declaration of Independence, the United States Constitution, the Articles of Confederation, and the state constitutions of Massachusetts, Connecticut, New Jersey, Pennsylvania, and Virginia. Republished in the *Gazeta de Caracas*, García de Sena's work was cited in the Venezuelan Congress and later widely distributed throughout Spanish America. In Uruguay, José Artigas became familiar with North American constitutional documents through García de Sena's translations. Artigas's "Instrucciones Orientales" to the delegates to the 1813 Constituent Assembly held in Buenos Aires were in large measure based on North American constitutional principles; his "Constitución Oriental" was inspired by the state constitution of Massachusetts. And in 1817, prior to his successful military campaign in Chile, General San Martín ordered the distribution of García de Sena's translations in the territories to be liberated.[17]

A number of other translations of North American constitutional documents were also made during this period, often having evident political influence. In 1811, Miguel de Pomba published at Bogotá the United States Constitution, the Articles of Confederation, and the Declaration of Independence. Camilio Torres's *Act of the Provinces of New Granada* drew its federal structure from the Articles of Confederation of the United States. A fragment of a translation of the United States Constitution, dated 1813, has been found in the papers of a member of the Paraguayan junta of that year. In Chile, Camilio Henríquez's revolutionary newspaper *Aurora de Chile* not only extensively discussed North American political ideas but published excerpts from Paine's *Common Sense*, Washington's Farewell Address, and Jefferson's first inaugural. In Buenos Aires, Manuel Belgrano and Mariano Moreno also quoted approvingly from Washington and Jefferson, and Moreno actually published his own modified Spanish version of the United States Constitution.[18]

In Mexico, the United States Constitution was serialized by the *Diario* as early as 1812. In the short time between Mexico's Declaration of Independence in 1821 and the adoption of a federal constitution in 1824, North American constitutional documents were published in large numbers. The Constitution appeared in the *Semanario Político y Literario* as well as in a published edition along with *Common Sense*, the Declaration of Independence, and the Articles of Confederation, under the title *Ideas necesarias a todo pueblo americano independiente que quiero ser libre (Ideas Necessary to All Independent People Who Wish to be Free)*. In 1823, *El Aguila Mexicana* published a comprehensive description of the United States which included a detailed treatment of the Massachusetts state constitution.[19]

Thus as Spanish Americans struggled to establish constitutional traditions, they naturally looked at the examples set by their neighbor to the north. Although North American constitutionalism was only one of several traditions that influenced the development of the independent Latin American nations, it was widely influential because it seemed to be responsive to certain desires of Spanish Americans: their intention to base their new nations on the principles of the Enlightenment, their aim to break with the legacy of Spanish administrative centralization, and their hope to create a polity that would encourage liberal social and economic development.

III

Although North American constitutional ideas were woven into the Spanish American political tradition, that process took place within certain specific political contexts. Throughout the region, independence brought in its wake not only physical destruction and economic crisis but also political conflict between competing elites. Constitutional formulations were not only matters of philosophical interest—they were matters of immediate political concern. At one extreme—as in the case of Mexico's Santa Anna—ideology was usually a matter of political convenience and a formulation to be changed as political conditions changed. But even discounting such individual cases, it is difficult to generalize about the internal political alignments of countries that have had markedly different historical experiences and social and economic conditions.

In Venezuela and the northern countries of South America, the politics of the independence period revolved around the person of Simón Bolívar. Bolívar dedicated himself to the defeat of the Spanish and the unity of Spanish America. But one commentator has suggested that though his greatest military enemies were Royalist troops, his greatest political foe was the influence of North American constitutionalism. Bolívar's attitudes toward, and use of, the North American political model, however, were a good deal more complicated than that formulation allows. His political philosophy was forged by the fortunes of war and the need to reconstruct authority. He ascribed a fatal weakness to the idea of federalism at a time when he felt strong leadership and unity were imperative.[20]

Bolívar's ideas about the constitutional structure of government were conditioned strongly by events. He attributed the failure and defeat of the First Venezuelan Republic, for example, to the political and constitutional weakness of the Venezuelan Constitution of 1811—a document strongly influenced by North American constitutional principles. Its "fatal adoption of the system of tolerance," he wrote, and its adherence to "poorly understood principles of humanity, which do not authorize governments to use force in order to liberate people who are ignorant of the value of their rights," was not suited to the immediate needs of winning independence. After his first, brief reconquest of Venezuela in 1813, Bolívar admonished the governor of the province of Barinas that he had not liberated Venezuela in order to reestablish the federalism of the First Republic. "Division of power," Bolívar wrote, "has never established and perpetuated governments—only concentration has infused respect." He consistently argued that the principles of federalism and the division of powers had to be abandoned in favor of the strengthening of central institutions and the union of the Venezuelan states into one indivisible republic.[21]

Bolívar's objections to the use of political principles derived from the experience of the United States also reflected his rejection of the faith held by many Spanish American liberals that laws alone could remake society. Like both Burke and Montesquieu, Bolívar insisted that laws needed to be suited to the experience of the people for whom they are made. He stressed the importance of cultural differences between the North American and Spanish American character. Because of those differences, he argued, Spanish America could not successfully adopt North American political institutions. The legislators who had adopted the 1811 Constitution, Bolívar said, "had yielded to the ill-considered pleadings of those men from the provinces who were captivated by the apparent brilliance of the happiness of the North American people, believing that the blessings they enjoy result exclusively from their form of government rather than from the character and customs of the citizens." Bolívar urged that a constitution be drafted on "the peculiar tutelary experience of the Venezuelan people" rather than on North American constitutional ideas.[22]

Bolívar's opposition to the use of North American constitutional ideas was reinforced by his cultural and political aversion to North Americans—an aversion conditioned by wartime events. In the darkest days of the Venezuelan struggle for independence, two North American ships had been captured supplying the Spanish, and the United States government had withheld recognition of Bolívar's government. He later wrote that he detested the North Americans "to such a degree that I would not want it said that a Colombian did anything the same way they do." Surveying the international situation in 1822, he described the United States as "a very rich and powerful nation, extremely warlike and capable of anything." Instead of the political influence of the United States, he favored that of Great Britain. Bolívar proposed that the republican features of the British Constitution be used as Spanish America's model—a hereditary senate modeled on the House of Lords and a strong executive modeled on the constitutional role of the British monarch.[23]

Yet even Bolívar, implacably opposed to the federalism of the North American model and deeply dissappointed by the actions of the United States, used examples drawn from the constitutional experience of the United States when it served his purpose of advancing strong executive power. In his critique of the divided executive of the 1811 Venezuelan Constitution, Bolívar favorably alluded to the constitutional powers of the president of the United States. Similarly, when presenting his draft of the Bolivian Constitution of 1826 to the Congress of Bolivia, he again pointed to the example of the American presidency. He also likened the power of the Bolivian president to name his own successor to the practice of the Virginia dynasty in passing the American presidency through the office of the Secretary of State.[24] Bolívar's references to these examples in no way signified a departure from his position of rejecting many of the basic principles of North American constitutionalism. But they are evidence of the important role North American constitutionalism played in providing positive and negative arguments for certain Spanish American political institutions.

While Bolívar ultimately failed in his efforts to impose unity through a strong central government and a strong executive, Chilean conservatives were able to do so by the early 1830s. Under the conservative Constitution of 1833, Chile compiled an enviable record of political stability throughout much of the nineteenth century. But with this development, Chile charted a course away from liberal constitutionalism. The political dissenter, Isidore Errázuriz, wrote that Chilean "political legislation changed direction completely in 1833. It left the path of American democracy in order to move closer to the mode of Constitutional Europe."[25]

In the first years of the Chilean struggle for independence, North American constitutional ideas exercised considerable influence on Chilean political thought. The general and widespread admiration of Chileans for Anglo-American institutions, which paralleled the anti-Spanish tenor of the independence movement, was reinforced by a sentiment of solidarity with the ex-colonies of North America. Chileans were well acquainted with the European sources of liberal constitutionalism; the United States Constitution was viewed as a successful embodiment of liberal political philosophy, and, as such, its influence was reinforced rather than rivaled by French constitutionalism and the liberal Spanish Constitution of 1812. Indeed, during the early years of independence, Chileans looked to the United States Constitution as a successful example of the liberal constitutional principle of a balance of powers.[26]

Most importantly, North American constitutional principles came to be closely associated with federalism in Chile. The displacement of Spanish colonial power touched off a struggle between the outlying provinces and the capital, Santiago. As early as 1811, the North American example was cited by the provinces in their struggle for equal representation. During the federalist ascendancy of the 1820s, federalism became closely identified with liberalism in general and opposition to strong national executive power in particular. At that time, liberals ascribed the origins of Chilean independence to the "archetype and example" of the "federal government of the North Americans." To Chilean liberals such as José Miguel Infante the evident economic and social success of the United States was due not to the character of its people but to its political principles. The application of those principles to Chile offered a means by which political, social, and economic relationships between Chile's elites could be reordered.[27]

The short period of federalist ascendancy during the 1820s in Chile was marked by increasingly chaotic conditions. The conservative reaction in 1829 focused squarely on expunging both federalism and liberalism from Chile. Federalism was attacked for dividing the earlier unity that presumably had existed in the country. The conservatives did not agree with Infante that society could or, for that matter, should be remade by constitutional means. The conservative reaction reversed the course of Chile's political development. Liberals had exalted the principle of the balance of powers and feared a strong executive; the conservative Constitution of 1833 was marked by an extremely strong president. As a result of the close identification of North American constitutionalism with federalism and liberalism, the debacle of the 1820s, and the consequent conservative reaction, North American constitutional principles exercised little influence in Chile's subsequent political development.[28]

Both Bolívar and the Chilean conservatives stressed the unsuitability of North American constitutionalism to Latin America because of the constraints of social conditions. Mexican conservatives like Lucas Alamán took the argument a step further by asserting that an independent Mexico had broken with its past by assuming alien liberal institutions. In the wake of the defeat of Mexico by the United States in 1847, the conservative critique of Mexican liberalism gained the initiative. Mexican liberals, it was said, presumably had no independent national values with which to confront the aggressor. In Mexico, "so far from God and so close to the United States," the conservative critique of liberalism was strengthened by the proximity of the United States.[29]

The structure of Mexican liberalism, however, was derived from much more than the example of the United States—important as that was as a symbol of liberal progress. The United States and its political institutions had been of keen interest to Mexican liberals. During the first generation of independence, the social and political institutions of the United States were frequently idealized in the writings of many Mexican liberals. José María Luis Mora, however, one of the principal architects of Mexican liberal thought, while admiring the political institutions of the United States found little in them that he considered directly applicable to Mexico's needs. Mora was influenced more directly by British and continental liberalism and utilitarian thought, particularly by the French constitutional liberalism of Benjamin Constant. Mora came to believe that Mexico's social and institutional conditions were more similar to those of Europe than to those of the United States.[30]

The Mexican Constitution of 1824, while similar to that of the United States in many respects, was also firmly rooted in European and Hispanic precedents. The liberal Spanish Constitution of 1812, Constant's constitutional liberalism, and the Mexican institution of provincial deputations all contributed to its liberal, federal structure. With faith in the efficacy of constitutional reforms fading by the 1830s, Mora and Mexican liberals turned even more directly to Hispanic precedents. They found the most relevant models for the reform program of 1833 in the reforms of Spain's Charles III and the Cortes of Cadíz. Mexican liberalism failed not because it was "alien" but because of the inherent contradiction between liberal commitment to individual liberty and the need to reform corporate privileges.[31]

The weaving of North American constitutional ideas into Spanish American political thought and institutions was also evident in the adoption of the Argentine Constitution of 1853. During the first years of independence, the influence of North American constitutional principles was subordinated to those of the French Revolution, as liberal *porteños* from Buenos Aires sought to assert their hegemony over the provinces through a unitary rather than federal government. The constitutions of 1811, 1815, and 1817, each with a unicameral legislature and a plural executive, were influenced most strongly by French ideas. North American constitutional ideas were circulating in the Argentine provinces, however. In 1817, General San Martín complained about the strong tendency to consider the United States as a political model. The unpromulgated constitutional drafts of 1819 and 1826, each with a bicameral legislature, single executive, and independent judiciary, were influenced by the example of the United States. In the discussions in 1826 alone, fifty references to the United States were made during the constitutional debates.[32]

With the onset in 1829 of the personal dictatorship of Juan Manuel de Rosas, who nominally represented the provinces in their struggle with Buenos Aires, constitutional experimentation in Argentina came to a halt for a full generation. Not until 1852, when the rival caudillo Urguiza overthrew Rosas, and a generation of exiles returned, were constitutional ideas again debated in Argentina. It was in the context of a search for a compromise between the forces that had rent the Argentine provinces and Buenos Aires for forty years and that had pitted the popular masses who had supported Rosas against the "enlightened minority" who supported liberal institutions that the drafters of the Argentine Constitution of 1853 turned to the federal system of the United States as their most appropriate model.[33]

Argentineans had long been acquainted with North American constitutional documents. They also knew the political history of the United States, not only from the documents translated by García de Sena in 1811, but also from the same author's *Concise History of the United States*, which included a comparative study of American state constitutions, as well as from various Spanish, French, and Portuguese translations of the *Federalist Papers*, de Toqueville's *Democracy in America*, and Joseph Story's *Commentaries on the Constitution of the United States*.[34]

More importantly, however, by the time the delegates met in Santa Fe in 1853, North American constitutional ideas had become interwoven with Argentine ones. Not only had North American constitutional principles become part of the Argentine tradition through the draft constitutions of 1819 and 1826 but also through the work of Argentina's leading political theorist, Juan Batista Alberdi. Alberdi wrote *Bases y puntos de partida para la organizacíon política de la República argentina (Bases and Points of Departure for the Political Organization of the Argentine Republic)* during his exile in Chile in 1852. Like the *Federalist Papers*, *Bases* was first offered as a series of political arguments in the daily press.

Alberdi compared the problems that faced Argentina in 1852 to those of the United States prior to 1787. "The mechanism of the general government of the United States offers us an idea of how to make practicable the association of the principles upon which the organization of the national government should be based," he wrote. Viewing North American constitutionalism as a model of a mixed system of government that could bind the opposing Argentine forces of federalism and centralism, Alberdi made frequent references to North American documentary sources. These included the Articles of Confederation, the Massachusetts constitution, the United States Constitution, the *Federalist*

Papers, and Story's *Commentaries*. He pointed to the recently acquired territory of California with its Hispanic population as proof that Argentina's problems could be remedied by the application of a similar constitutional system.[35]

It is difficult to disentangle the influence that North American constitutional documents exercised at the Santa Fe convention from that of Alberdi's work. One delegate reported that the *Federalist Papers* had been available in the office of the secretary of the convention during the preparatory sessions, "but when the moment came to draft the Constitution the book had disappeared." The loss was considered "irreparable" by the delegates, until they learned of Alberdi's *Bases*, which "fixed the path to be followed in drafting the constitution."[36]

It is quite evident, however, that the example of the United States was clearly in the minds of the delegates. In the debates at Santa Fe, members of the committee that drafted the constitution, as well as the president of the convention, noted that the draft was modeled on the United States Constitution. When the Province of Buenos Aires, which did not attend the Santa Fe convention, held a provincial convention in 1860 to consider accepting the 1853 Constitution, the deliberations were influenced by North American precedents to an even greater extent than had been the Santa Fe convention. More than 168 references were made during the convention to the United States Constitution and to the political and economic history of the United States. The delegates believed that Argentina's political and economic conditions were similar to those of the United States and felt that the province of Buenos Aires should ground its joining of the Argentine federation on the basis of the principles of the United States Constitution—"the only authoritative constitution in the world whose essence cannot be altered without violating the basic principles of federalism."[37]

But the Argentine Constitution of 1853 was by no means a carbon copy of the United States Constitution. As the noted Argentinean historian, José Luis Romero, has observed, although ideas have been imported, they have been "marked by a special stamp or, in other words, have assumed a halo of peculiar tones—a reflection of the conditions under which we live." Although the mechanism of federalism may have been borrowed, the necessity and conditions that occasioned its use were Argentine in character. Just as the United States Constitution was itself the product of compromise between conflicting tendencies within the thirteen North American states, so the Argentine Constitution of 1853 was a response to conflicting forces within the Argentine provinces: it was shaped by Argentine conditions.[38]

Both procedurally and substantively, the federalism of the 1853 Constitution veered strongly towards central authority, a position liberals had always favored in Argentina. Although Argentineans accepted the principle of the separation of the legislative and constituent powers, the Santa Fe convention exercised legislative, executive, and electoral functions in addition to its constituent powers—unlike the Philadelphia convention of 1787. Unlike the North American precedent, also, the Argentine Constitution was not submitted to provincial conventions for ratification but became effective when approved by the convention and proclaimed by the provisional director.[39]

Substantively, there were significant differences between the relation of the Argentine central government and the provinces as compared to that established by the United States Constitution. Under the Argentine Constitution, the central government was given a much more extensive ability and power to intervene in provincial affairs. This outcome reflected Alberdi's influence. He rejected the more liberal and federal aspects of North American constitutionalism in favor of Hamiltonian centralism. This emphasis was due not only to the traditional affinity of Argentine liberalism for centralized authority but also to its commitment to the use of political institutions as agencies of economic development.[40]

The use of federalism in Argentina as an instrument of national integration and social and economic development was well illustrated by the career of one of Alberdi's contemporaries, Domingo Faustino Sarmiento, President of Argentina from 1868 through 1874. Sarmiento made his literary reputation during his exile in Chile in the 1840s when he wrote *El Facundo*, a searing attack on the tyranny of Rosas. Sarmiento fervently admired the social and political institutions of the United States, particularly American common schools. He wanted Argentina to overcome its "barbaric" Hispanic heritage and as president did not hesitate to use the full range of powers given the national government. In fact, he frequently resorted to extralegal means when he deemed it necessary to the success of policies he considered imperative. Sarmiento was the first Argentine political leader to base his claims to legitimacy not on local prominence but on an "immense personal following" throughout the nation. He did not present himself as the champion of a single region or group but as the "provincial who is accepted in Buenos Aires." Although Sarmiento did not change the structure of Argentine politics from its essential personalism, he was instrumental in changing its focus from provincial to national concerns and thereby furthered the process of national integration that began at Santa Fe in 1853.[41]

Despite the significant differences between Argentinean federalism and that of the United States, the influence of North American constitutionalism was far more than simply cosmetic. The development of the Argentine federal judiciary—long one of the strongest and most independent judiciaries in Latin America—showed the continuing and substantive influence of North American constitutional ideas. Argentine legislators used precedents drawn from the United States, particularly the Judiciary Act of 1789, when organizing the Argentine federal judiciary. Like the United States Constitution, the Argentine Constitution did not explictly authorize judicial review of legislative and executive acts. But the Argentine Court exercised the power on the basis that the intent of the framers of the constitution had been to model the Argentine federal courts on those of the United States and that by 1853 the power of judicial review had long been established in the United States. In deciding substantive cases the Argentine Court often turned to statements of North American legal doctrines and precedents, particularly the *Federalist Papers*, Story's *Commentaries*, Kent's *Commentaries on American Law*, and a collection of United States legal decisions translated by Nicolas Calvo and Clodomiro Quirogo.[42]

IV

The influence of North American constitutionalism in nineteenth-century Spanish America was part of the broader influence of political and economic liberalism. The most powerful reason for the influence of North American constitutional ideas was the evident social and economic progress of the United States. To Spanish Americans, North American constitutionalism was not a model to be simply copied but a model of what political and economic liberalism could accomplish within a specific context. On that basis, it became one of the major strands from which Latin American liberalism was fashioned.

The influence of North American constitutionalism also operated within the broader context of the deeply ambivalent attitude of Spanish Americans to the colossus of the North. The recognition of social and cultural differences between the United States and Hispanic America and the need to differentiate Spanish America politically and culturally from the overwhelming presence of the North weighed against the admiration for North American political institutions.

Much of the Spanish American ambivalence toward the United States and its political institutions was captured in José Martí's account of the celebration in Philadelphia during the centennial of the United States Constitution. Writing for publication in Latin American newspapers, Martí took pains to point out that in 1787, "Philadelphia experienced the same frenzies, discords, and strifes which Latins in their ignorance and their sickly inordinate admiration" of North Americans considered to be a condition unique to Latin America. Martí's rendition of the events of the Philadelphia convention of 1787 was offered to his readers as evidence that "the North American becomes impassioned, exalted, rebellious, confused, corrupt even as the Hispanic American does."[43]

Martí, whose cultural aversion to North American ways is well known, did not want Latin Americans to emulate the product of the Philadelphia convention: what he pointed to as worthy of emulation was the process of political accommodation of discordant interests that it represented and the social and economic progress that it had brought. To Martí, the lesson that North American constitutionalism taught the world was this: "Only the forms of government that are born within a nation take root in it, and that even as the Articles of Confederation fell into disuse and ridicule because they were imitations of the Greek leagues, likewise foreign purple can rot a cloth ill-fitted to receive it, and needing perhaps no other colors than those the native sun will shed upon it." In the final analysis the most significant event of the centennial celebration to Martí was the industrial pageant: it "showed industries as they were a hundred years ago, wretched, rustic, on donkey back, and as they are now.... Never have men advanced more in a hundred years, because never was liberty so real."[44]

The promise of nineteenth-century liberalism—social and economic progress—failed to materialize in Latin America. Yet its failure should not be allowed to obscure the important contributions that it made to the Latin American political tradition. What economic progress did occur was uneven, increased social tensions, and was heavily dependent on foreign sources and markets.[45] The revolutionary Mexican Constitution of 1917, which became a leading influence on subsequent Latin American constitutions, went beyond the confines of nineteenth-century political and economic liberalism in its attempt to address Mexico's social and economic problems.[46] Few observers today can share the faith in the efficacy of political and constitutional reform that was held by many nineteenth-century liberals.[47]

Any assessment of the significance of the influence of North American constitutionalism in Spanish America can only be undertaken as part of a broader effort to determine the relevance of liberalism to the historical development of Latin America. One close student of the Latin American political tradition, Claudio Véliz, has argued that nineteenth-century liberalism was a "pause" within an overall tradition of centralism and authoritarianism. And Glen Dealy has argued cogently that at no time did Spanish Americans embrace the basic assumptions of political liberalism. Dealy has shown that nineteenth-century constitutions typically included numerous provisions derived from Hispanic traditions that were at variance with basic liberal principles.[48]

Nineteenth-century Spanish American liberalism no doubt bore the marks of its own cultural and political traditions, particularly in the relationships between church and state and between the executive and legislative powers. Spanish American liberals generally acknowledged Roman Catholicism as the religion of the state. And Spanish American presidents wielded far greater constitutional powers, particularly in the initiation and enactment of law, than did the presidents of the United States.[49]

But to dismiss the significance of liberalism as either ephemeral or as a mirage belies the complexity of the historical development of Latin America. To do so underestimates the degree to which liberalism did achieve a substantial legitimacy within Spanish American political culture as well as the important role of geographic, economic, and social differences within the Latin American historical experience. While Spanish American liberals accepted the religious role of the Catholic Church, the most crucial distinction that separated them from conservatives was the desire of the liberals to circumscribe the political role of the Church. And the constitutional dominance of the executive, initially based on the needs to mobilize against Spain and to gain the confidence of European governments, was necessitated by the need to overcome archaic social institutions and to integrate nation-states. Frank Safford has recently suggested that even the frequent extra-constitutional actions of the elite were tied to their revolutionary task of overthrowing Spanish social, economic, and political institutions in favor of new ones based on British, French, and North American models.[50] Liberalism, and, by extension, North American constitutionalism, was an important part—but only a part—of a continuing political process that of necessity has responded to both Latin American culture and conditions and to broad political currents within the world of which Latin America is a part. In the early nineteenth century, that world, as Peggy Liss has shown, was the Atlantic "network," and Latin America's development was part of the political development of that broader network.[51]

The experience of Latin America with nineteenth-century liberalism was a significant part of its historical experience. It continues to exert an influence: the traveller to Mexico City today is not long in discovering the continuing symbolic importance of Benito Juárez and the Constitution of 1857—heirs to the liberalism of Mora's generation—to contemporary Mexican political culture. Few observers appreciate the strong role in the Latin American political tradition played by the liberal tradition of individual freedoms and strong judiciaries or of the tradition of no reelection of presidents.[52]

Most importantly, consideration of the Spanish American experience points to the need to address the full complexity of political and constitutional developments when assessing the influence of North American constitutionalism abroad. North American constitutional documents were only one of numerous sources that Spanish Americans turned to when framing their constitutions. North American constitutionalism was influential precisely because it embodied values and addressed needs shared by many Spanish Americans. Its influence was not unique but operated within the broad spectrum of ideas available to Spanish Americans. In Spanish America, the influence of North American constitutionalism was bound intimately with the broader set of beliefs, attitudes, and perceptions that characterized relations between the Americas, as well as with its association with specific social and political interests and the current of nineteenth-century liberalism.

NOTES

The author would like to thank Peggy Liss for an instructive reading of an earlier draft.

1. For one of the most recent interpretations that emphasizes the contradiction, see Claudio Véliz, *The Centralist Tradition of Latin America* (Princeton, N.J.: Princeton University Press, 1980); more specifically related to the influence of constitutional ideas is J. Lloyd Mecham, "Latin American Constitutions: Nominal and Real," *Journal of Politics* 21 (1959): 258–75. While qualifying the assessment, Russell Fitzgibbon agreed that in the nineteenth century, "Latin American constitutions failed to be the creatures of their own environment; they were simply alien adoptions and adaptations." "Constitutional Development in Latin America: A Synthesis," *American Political Science Review* 39 (1945): 521.

2. John Lynch, "The Origins of Spanish American Independence," in Leslie Bethel, ed., *The Cambridge History of Latin America* (Cambridge: Cambridge University Press, 1985), 3:42–46; Frank Safford, "Politics, Ideology and Society in Post-Independence Spanish America," *Cambridge History of Latin America* 3:355–58; Arthur P. Whitaker, ed., *Latin America and the Enlightenment*, 2nd ed. (Ithaca, N.Y.: Cornell University Press, 1961), particularly the essays by Harry Bernstein, "Some Inter-American Aspects of the Enlightenment," and Charles C. Griffin, "The Enlightenment and Latin American Independence"; Peggy Liss, *Atlantic Empires: The Network of Trade and Revolution, 1713–1826* (Baltimore, Md.: Johns Hopkins University Press, 1983), 158; Abelardo Levaggi, "Origen del poder legislativo en hispanoamérica (1810–1814)," *Revista del Instituto de Historia del Derecho Ricardo Levene* 19 (1968): 30–63 assesses twenty-seven constitutional texts of the period, detailing Anglo-Saxon, French, and Spanish influences.

3. Lynch, "Origins," *Cambridge History of Latin America* 3:46–47; Santos P. Amadeo, *Argentine Constitutional Law: The Judicial Function in the Maintenance of the Federal System and the Preservation of Individual Rights* (New York: Columbia University Press, 1943), 11–20; Charles Hale, *Mexican Liberalism in the Age of Mora, 1821–1853* (New Haven: Yale University Press, 1968); Nettie Lee Benson, *La disputación provincial y el federalismo mexicano* (Mexico City: El Colegio de Mexico, 1955) and "Spain's Contributions to Federalism in Mexico," in Thomas E. Cotner and Carlos E. Castenada, eds., *Essays in Mexican History* (Austin: University of Texas Press, 1958), 90–103; Victor Andrés Belaunde, *Bolívar and the Political Thought of the Spanish American Revolution* (Baltimore, Md.: Johns Hopkins University Press, 1938), 216; Simon Collier, *Ideas and Politics of Chilean Independence* (Cambridge: Cambridge University Press, 1967), 152, 176, 201–6; and Arthur P. Whitaker, *The Western Hemisphere Idea: Its Rise and Decline* (Ithaca, N.Y.: Cornell University Press, 1954).

4. Cited in William Spence Robertson, *Hispanic-American Relations with the United States* (New York: Oxford University Press, 1923), 72. In general, see José Luis Romero, "La independencia de hispano américa y el modelo político norteamericano," *Inter-American Review of Bibliography* 26 (1976): 429–55; Belaunde, *Political Thought*, 148–51; and Robertson, *Hispanic-American Relations*, 72–73, 81–82. Also see Javier Ocampo Lopez, "La agitación revolucionaria en el Nuevo Reino de Granada y el ejemplo de la independencia de Estado Unidos," *Revista de Historia de América* (Instituto Panamericano de Geografía e Historia, Comisión de Historia, Mexico) 82 (1976): 29–52, which details attempts to apply the federal model in Colombia during the first years of independence; William Marion Gibson, *The Constitutions of Colombia* (Durham, N.C.: Duke University Press, 1948), which is a convenient source in which to trace the continuing federalist-centralist polarity in Colombian constitutional history; Joedd Price, "Images and Influences: The Legacy of the Founding Fathers and the Federal System in Ecuador," *Latin American Research Review* 10 (1975): 121–36, shows the influence of federalism and the political example of the United States between 1830 and 1845; and Hale, *Mexican Liberalism*, 194.

5. See Collier, *Chilean Independence*, 316–17 for examples of contemporary criticisms; see Véliz, *The Centralist Tradition*, for one of the most recent criticisms.

6. Romero, "El modelo político norteamericano"; Benson, "Federalism in Mexico," 90; Stanley J. and Barbara H. Stein, *The Colonial Heritage of Latin America: Essays on Economic Dependence in Perspective* (New York: Oxford University Press, 1970), 133, 167, 170.

7. Safford, "Politics, Ideology, and Society," *Cambridge History of Latin America* 3:358, 383–84, 404–12, 418; David Bushnell, "The Independence of Spanish South America," *Cambridge History of Latin America* 3:110; Collier, *Chilean Independence*, 305–9; Benson, "Federalism in Mexico," 90; and Romero, "El modelo político norteamericano." For a wide ranging interpretation emphasizing the links between Latin American political theory and Latin America's place in the context of world trade in the eighteenth and early nineteenth centuries, see Liss, *Atlantic Empires*.

8. Cited in Collier, *Chilean Independence*, 302, 313; Bernard Moses, *The Intellectual Background of the Revolution in South America, 1810–1824* (New York: Hispanic Society of America, 1926), 9. Also see Gene H. Brack, *Mexico Views Manifest Destiny, 1821–1846: An Essay on the Origins of the Mexican War* (Albuquerque: University of New Mexico Press, 1975), 25, for similar sentiments by Mexicans.

9. Liss, *Atlantic Empires*, 32, 47, 109–24.

10. Collier, *Chilean Independence*, 37–39; Arthur P. Whitaker, *The United States and the Independence of Latin America* (Baltimore, Md.: Johns Hopkins University Press, 1941), 13–14; also see Roy F. Nichols, *Advance Agents of American Destiny* (Philadelphia: University of Pennsylvania Press, 1956).

11. Romero, "El modelo político norteamericano"; Robertson, *Hispanic-American Relations*, 63–6; William R. Manning, *Diplomatic Correspondence of the United States Concerning the Independence of the Latin American Nations*, 3 vols. (New York: Oxford University Press, 1925), 1:655, 2:923–24; and J. Lloyd Mecham, "Origins of Federalism in Mexico," in Conyers Read, ed., *The Constitution Reconsidered* (New York: Columbia University Press, 1938), 361.

12. J. Fred Rippy, *Joel R. Poinsett, Versatile American* (Durham, N.C.: Duke University Press, 1935), vii, 35–57, 104–34, instructions cited 106; and Collier, *Chilean Independence*, 97–98, 112, 307.

13. Rippy, *Poinsett*, 35–57, 104–34; Collier, *Chilean Independence*, 97–98, 112, 307; and Brack, *Mexico Views Manifest Destiny*, 44, 28–37.

14. D. A. G. Waddell, "International Politics and Latin American Independence," *Cambridge History of Latin America* 3:204, 219; Liss, *Atlantic Empires*, 109, 123–24; and Reginald Horsman, *Race and Manifest Destiny: The Origins of American Racial Anglo-Saxonism* (Cambridge, Mass.: Harvard University Press, 1981), chapter 6.

15. Horsman, *Race and Manifest Destiny*; and Brack, *Mexico Views Manifest Destiny*, 15, 44–45, 169.

16. Robertson, *Hispanic-American Relations*, 64.

17. Romero, "El modelo político norteamericano"; Robertson, *Hispanic-American Relations*, 71, 84–86; Belaunde, *Political Thought*, 151; and Collier, *Chilean Independence*, 174.

18. Robertson, *Hispanic-American Relations*, 75–77, 80–84; Javier Ocampo López, *La independencia de los Estados Unidos de America y su proyección en Hispanoamérica: el modelo norteamericano y su repercusión en la independencia de Colombia; un estudio a través de la folletería de la independencia de Colombia* (Caracas: Instituto Panamericano de Geografía e Historia, Comisión de Historia, Comité Orígenes de la Emancipación, 1979) includes an essay on the United States Constitution by Miguel de Pombo as an appendix; Eduardo Durnhofer, *Mayo y el antecedente norteamericano* (Buenos Aires: Instituto Bonaerense de Numismática y Antigüedades, 1976) reproduces and comments on Moreno's modified version of the United States Constitution; also see Sylvia Fridman and María Inés Soulés, "The Influence of American Thought in the Revolutionary Movement of Argentina's River Plate, 1810–1820: A Bibliographic Essay," *American Studies International* 18 (1981): 45–62.

19. Robertson, *Hispanic-American Relations*, 65; and Brack, *Mexico Views Manifest Destiny*, 18, 23–25.

20. *Selected Writings of Bolívar*, comp. Vicente Lecuna, ed. Harold A. Bierck, Jr., tr. Lewis Bertrand, 2 vols. (New York: The Colonial Press, 1951), 1: xx; cf. Liss, *Atlantic Empires*, 218–21.

21. Ibid. 1:15, 18, 45–46, 179–81, 190, 192, 194.

22. Ibid. 1:177–80; also see 2:729.

23. Ibid. 1:185–89, 307; 2:541; Liss, *Atlantic Empires*, 218–21, and 216–17 for discussion of similar events and reactions in Chile and Argentina.

24. Ibid. 1:180; 2:596–606.

25. Collier, *Chilean Independence*, 354.

26. Ibid., 152, 176, 201–6.

27. Ibid., 302–13; and Robertson, *Hispanic-American Relations*, 81–82.

28. Collier, *Chilean Independence*, 205–6, 316–17, 336–37, 345–46, 354.

29. Safford, "Politics, Ideology and Society," *Cambridge History of Latin America*, 3:397; and Hale, *Mexican Liberalism*, 16–17, 32, 303.

30. Hale, *Mexican Liberalism*, 73, 92, 95, 178, 189, 195–96, 202–3, 302–3. See especially chapters 2 and 3. Hale discounts the importance of North American constitutional documents in the early 1820s.

31. Ibid., chapter 3 and pp. 39, 111–13, 147, 193.

32. Robertson, *Hispanic-American Relations*, 86–89; Amadeo, *Argentine Constitutional Law*, 8–12, 15–20. Also see Belaunde, *Political Thought*, 27–31; and Romero, "El modelo político norteamericano," for discussions of competing political influences.

33. José Luis Romero, *A History of Argentine Political Thought*, tr. Thomas F. McGann (Stanford: Stanford University Press, 1963), 60; also see 149–54. On Rosas, see John Lynch, *Argentine Dictator: Juan Manuel de Rosas, 1829–1852* (Oxford, England: Clarendon Press, 1981).

34. Amadeo, *Argentine Constitutional Law*, 28, 32–33.

35. Leon G. Campbell, "The Politics of Preparation: A Comparison of the Political Thought of Alexander Hamilton and Juan Batista Alberdi," *Revista/Review Interamericana* 4 (1974): 87; Robertson, *Hispanic-American Relations*, 89–96; and Amadeo, *Argentine Constitutional Law*, 31–32.

36. Amadeo, *Argentine Constitutional Law*, 29–30.

37. Ibid. 33–34, 36–38.

38. Romero, *Argentine Political Thought*, 3–4, 60, 149–54; and Amadeo, *Argentine Constitutional Law*, 7–11.

39. Amadeo, *Argentine Constitutional Law*, 34–36, 44.

40. Ibid. 88–97; Romero, "El modelo político norteamericano"; and Campbell, "Alberdi and Hamilton," 88–91.

41. Allison Bunkley, *The Life of Sarmiento* (Princeton, N.J.: Princeton University Press, 1952), 216, 346, 356, 396, 399, 462–63, 472–73. Also see Sarmiento's *Travels in the United States in 1847*, tr. Michael Aaron Rockland (Princeton, N.J.: Princeton University Press, 1970).

42. Amadeo, *Argentine Constitutional Law*, 49, 63–64, 73–75, 85–87.

43. José Martí, "Centennial of the Constitution," in *Martí on the U.S.A.*, ed. and tr. Luis A. Baralt (Carbondale: Southern Illinois University Press, 1965), 125.

44. Ibid. 128, 135–37.

45. The literature is voluminous. As a starting point, see E. Bradford Burns, *The Poverty of Progress: Latin America in the Nineteenth Century* (Berkeley: University of California Press, 1980).

46. Even the Mexican Constitution of 1917 did not constitute a total break with the liberal principles of the constitutions of 1824 and 1857. See E. Victor Niemeyer, *Revolution at Queretaro: The Mexican Constitutional Convention of 1916–1917* (Austin: University of Texas Press, 1974).

47. In the twentieth century the United States has often tended to view Latin American social and economic problems as rooted in political maldevelopment and has attempted to transfer North American legal and institutional models to Latin America. Although the efforts continue, the history is one of failure. For documentation of the failure of an attempt to transfer American legal models to Brazil, Chile, and Colombia in the 1960s and 1970s, see James A. Gardner, *Legal Imperialism: American Lawyers and Foreign Aid in Latin America* (Madison: University of Wisconsin Press, 1980).

48. Véliz, *The Centralist Tradition*; Dealy, "Prolegomena on the Spanish American Political Tradition," *Hispanic American Historical Review* 48 (1968): 37–58.

49. Leslie Bethell, "A Note on the Church and the Independence of Latin

America," *Cambridge History of Latin America* 3:209–33; and Jacques Lambert, *Latin America: Social Structures and Political Institutions*, tr. Helen Katel (Berkeley: University of California Press, 1967), 16–20, 217–20, 320–44.

50. Bethell, "Note," *Cambridge History of Latin America* 3:209–33; Lambert, *Latin America*, 16–20, 217–20, 260, 320–44; and Safford, "Politics, Ideology and Society," *Cambridge History of Latin America* 3:359, 370, 413–17.

51. Liss, *Atlantic Empires*.

52. See especially Charles Hale, "The Reconstruction of Nineteenth-Century Politics in Spanish America: A Case for the History of Ideas," *Latin American Research Review* 8 (1973): 53–73; and Lambert, *Latin America* 18: 272–96, 324–33.

3

American Constitutionalism and the Emergence of a Liberal World Order

Peter S. Onuf and Nicholas G. Onuf

The following essay differs in perspective and approach from the other pieces in this volume. It stresses intellectual history somewhat more and analyzes the ideas of two men—Henry Wheaton and William Ladd. The Onufs argue that Americans were interested in bringing about a more liberal world order based on international law and the peace movement, rather than in establishing a tradition of American constitutionalism as such. They reverse the emphasis found in the previous essays, in other words, by focusing their discussion within America rather than on the effects and responses abroad. In this way they suggest a different sphere for studying the influence of American constitutionalism in its inception as well as in its results.

Henry Wheaton's *Elements of International Law*, first published in 1836, remained the most influential statement of international legal doctrine for many decades. The *Elements* went through numerous editions and translations throughout the nineteenth century, setting the pattern for rival treatises that eventually crowded the field. It was not until 1880, when William E. Hall's *A Treatise on International Law* appeared, or even 1905, with the publication of Lassa Oppenheim's *International Law*, that it was superseded as the leading English language text.[1]

The wide influence of Wheaton's treatise raises a number of intriguing questions for students of emergent liberal internationalism. Why was Wheaton's conception of world order so attractive—all over the world—to promoters of an international regime of law? What particular ideological or doctrinal predispositions did Wheaton, as an American legal writer and diplomat, bring to his work? These questions are of more than antiquarian or provincial interest. It is the premise of this chapter that a close reading of Wheaton's text offers important clues to the development of liberal conceptions of world order. In the process, we hope to correct the prevailing misinterpretations of the genealogy of "positivist" and "naturalist" elements in contemporary international legal thought. Our reading of Wheaton thus requires a reconsideration of the classic treatises.

In the organization of their texts as well as in their doctrinal commitments, writers like Wheaton sought to impose order on the diffuse, often contradictory, practices constituting "international society." Wheaton and his fellow liberals sought to create an international legal regime in which formally equal, sovereign states would pursue their independent, but ultimately harmonious interests in a rational, systematic fashion. The relation to the domestic economy is clear: liberal internationalists expected the world system to gain increasing rationality through the spread of commerce—and therefore of complementary interests—and through the international division of labor.

If Henry Wheaton was the first great systematizer of the working order of the liberal century, William Ladd was his counterpart in imagining a reformed world order. As founder of the American Peace Society in 1828, Ladd is the central figure in a peace movement that rapidly spread through progressive circles in the United States and Britain. Insofar as Ladd and his followers found the liberal order wanting, their response was to consider ways of making it work better—which is to say, more rationally—in achieving liberal objectives of peace and prosperity. The peace movement lost most of its energy by the 1850s. Yet it markedly reinforced the liberal predilection for arbitration as the preferred mode for settling disputes: by codification of international law to reduce uncertainty and opportunism, and by marshalling public opinion against the intemperate or unenlightened conduct of nation-states.

To a large extent, liberal assumptions still shape the way we see the world. Indeed, the order that nineteenth-century liberal writers believed was immanent in—though sometimes obscured by—the confusion of contemporary state practice now seems to late- and post-liberal theorists to be a willful misrepresentation of the realities of world power. Yet nineteenth-century liberals, for whom the conception of a coherent world order was necessarily an act of bold imagining, had no misgivings about the reality of the order they uncovered and helped to create. These positivist seekers of truth-in-"facts" were confident that systematic analysis would yield lawful regularities in international behavior that were at once descriptive and normative. Latter-day critics rejected this naive rationalism with its scientific pretensions demonstrating that liberals persistently confused legal principle and ideological preference. The assumption that sovereign states are "equal" is now seen as an absurd distortion of world power relations. But whether or not there is a "real" world behind the "liberal world order," that order certainly exists, both in the minds of believers and in the institutions and practices that it calls into being and then describes. These liberal realities resist easy demystification.

Our task is to reconstruct the premises of liberal internationalism at the time of its birth. Wheaton's *Elements of International Law* provides a point of departure. We will show that English Utilitarians did not exercise the preponderant influence on Wheaton—any more than on Ladd or on nineteenth-century conceptions of world order generally—that is usually assumed. Instead, we argue, Wheaton's approach to international law draws more on Emmerich de Vattel and, through Vattel, on Christian Wolff. But these literary influences were less important to Wheaton than the American experience with the world, beginning with the founding generation. A full explication of *The Elements* must go beyond simple textual comparisons to grasp the distinctively American vision of world peace through law that Wheaton shared with Ladd and articulated, like Ladd, on the world's behalf. Indeed, we will argue, the thrust of American liberalism, beginning in the Revolutionary era, was precisely in their direction: Americans believed that the world-historical significance of their Revolution would be realized in its transforming impact on international society.

I

Many Americans believed that the independence of the United States would transform international relations; they were less confident that their example would—or should—have a direct impact on constitutional development elsewhere. Americans saw themselves playing a crucial role in reforming state practice—notably in commercial treaties and in promoting alternatives to war, most conspicuously in the arbitration movement—and in rationalizing these reforms through treatise writing and codification. The most enduring and consequential impact of American independence, therefore, was not supposed to be on political or constitutional development in other nations but rather on the liberalization of world order. American constitutional innovations were widely influential during the "age of the democratic revolution" but had less of an impact on the organization of European polities thereafter.[2] Disenchantment with the French Revolution and the coincidental rejection of natural rights doctrine discouraged constitutional innovation and strengthened the hold of existing regimes. Many Europeans—and Americans for that matter—were convinced that political liberty flourished in the United

States only because of exceptional conditions, notably the broad availability of landed property. American "exceptionalists" thus did not see America as the wave of the future, but as a fortunate exemption from the laws of social and political development.[3]

What was America's significance for emergent liberalism, if it were not as a paradigm for state structure? Enlightenment political economists welcomed the American Revolution as a blow against colonialism. They believed colonialism distorted the world system in much the same way that state-sanctioned monopoly privileges distorted domestic economies.[4] Though the Revolution may have been seen as a rejection of monarchy—and monarchy could be seen as the "constitutional" cause of the misguided foreign policies that obstructed free trade and kept the world at war—European liberals were hesitant to conclude that revolutions in their own countries were necessary. Instead, enlightened government in the New World provided a model for reform that even monarchs would find irresistible because of its obvious material advantages. Existing regimes could redeem themselves by recognizing the new nation and participating in the new world order it had inaugurated.

European commentators recognized that the American Revolution initiated a new epoch in world history, but this "newness" was not necessarily or primarily in state structure. Instead, the independence of the United States transformed world order. Edmund Burke wrote:

> A great revolution has happened [in America]—a revolution made not by chopping and changing of power in any of the existing states, but by the appearance of a new state, of a new species, in a new part of the globe. It has made as great a change in all the relations, and balances, and gravitations of power, as the appearance of a new planet would in the system of the solar world.[5]

Even before the union was reconstituted, a writer in the *Liverpool Advertiser* could report, "we every where discern the influence of the great revolution across the Atlantic on commerce, on the balance of power, and the genius of nations."[6]

Cosmopolitan Americans responded to and exploited Enlightenment expectations by emphasizing their contributions to the transformation of international society. Recognition of the new nation was itself an implicit endorsement of the new world order. Meanwhile, beginning with the "model treaty" of 1776, the revolutionaries sought to revolutionize diplomacy.[7] Forward-looking Americans already entertained notions of their "manifest destiny" to expand across the continent.[8] The organization of a federal system under the new constitution suggested that a state system could be rationally and realistically organized in order to eliminate war and promote economic development. Benjamin Franklin was a tough-minded realist, but he believed that the law of nations would be effectively implemented in the new federal republic.[9] The United States would transform the world by its enlightened participation in international society and by the example of institutions it developed for adjusting claims and interests among "sovereign" states.

In James Madison's opinion, the "frequency of wars" in the past could be attributed to "a will in the government independent of the will of the people."[10] Because the American government now represented the people, they would no longer be drawn into interimperial wars, as they had been throughout the colonial period. A New York writer asserted that, "little or no analogy [now] holds between the new and the old world.... We have no Continental connections. No Monarch to support in his mad schemes of ambition. No Colonies to subjugate."[11] The interests and inclinations of the people were always peaceful. In Europe governments preyed not only on their own people but, through wars, on the people of other countries. To end the rule of kings would be to empower the naturally noncombatant and to permit the true national interest—the "happiness" of the people—to determine policy.

But few Americans believed that the republican millennium was imminent; this "realism" was central to their view of the world. Recognizing that kings elsewhere were unlikely to lay down their crowns immediately, Franklin suggested that nations (and kings themselves) take steps to minimize the scope of monarchical ambition. They should agree that in any future war farmers, fishermen, merchants, and mechanics "should be undisturbed, have the Protections of both Sides, and be permitted to follow their Employments in Surety." Given such guarantees, that "Encouragement to War which arises from a Spirit of Rapine, would be taken away."[12] In Franklin's vision, the world could become "republican" *before* the governments of particular states were reconstituted along republican lines. A more peaceful, liberal world order would be achieved by positive agreements among states, not by revolutionary regime changes.

Many Americans seconded English liberal Richard Price's flattering prediction in his *Observations on the Importance of the American Revolution* (1784) that American independence could lead toward "universal peace" and an end to "all war."[13] But they also agreed with Price that it was only a tentative first step. Americans would have to secure their own union and thus "prevent future wars among themselves" before they could fulfill their world-historical destiny.[14] When Price wrote, the issue seemed uncertain at best. The English press was flooded with reports of anarchy and interstate conflict in the new nation.[15] In a letter to Price, included in the *Observations*, Turgot, the French economist, warned that the disintegration of the union would unleash a flood of violence: America would become "an image of our Europe, a mass of divided powers contending for territory and commerce."[16]

Though the United States as a nation might not be warlike in relation to the rest of the world, Americans could easily find themselves in a state of nature—or war—with each other. The absence of effective order on a continental scale would inexorably lead to a counterrevolutionary reaction. The preservation of order in the New World depended on strengthening the union and achieving economic as well as political independence. Postwar disputes between states and sections—and the outbreak of mob violence—demonstrated that republicanism alone was hardly sufficient to immunize America from conflict. To keep the peace among sovereign states, it would be necessary to establish effective institutions for resolving controversies, particularly over jurisdictional claims.[17]

Sympathetic Europeans agreed with their American friends that the success of this experiment in interstate organization could have a profound impact on the way the world itself might be organized in the future. A stronger union would simultaneously guarantee order among the American states and enable America to participate more effectively in promoting a more liberal world order. By expanding the scope of positive international law, treaties, conventions, and other international agreements would begin to create for the world at large the systematic, rational, stable conditions that the American states supposedly enjoyed. But an imperfect union belied the promise of order at home and abroad. As long as Congress was unable to compel Americans to comply with treaty commitments—as it was under the Articles of Confederation—the United States represented a destabilizing force and a vacuum of effective power. The inability to honor national obligations invited foreign intervention and jeopardized American independence.

The paradox implicit in postwar prescriptions for constitutional reform was that they suggested that the United States would have to take on the conventional *form* of a European state if it were to preserve the New World "empire of liberty" and not revert to Old World despotism. Reformers argued that national respectability was not only a realistic necessity—in a world infested with Algerine "pirates," hostile frontier "savages," and bitter commercial rivals—but that it was the means through which the promise of the Revolution would be redeemed. It was in this spirit that English liberal Thomas Pownall counselled the "Sovereigns of America" to translate the "abstract idea" of republican government into reality and thus "lift up on high a Standard to the Nations." To do this the American nation "must come forward amongst the Nations, as an active Existing Agent, a Personal Being, standing on the same ground as all other Personal Sovereigns."[18]

From the American perspective the success of the liberal project depended on expanding national power in order to participate effectively in international society. Only by making itself "respectable" abroad and by developing its own vast economic potential could the new nation extend its benign, liberalizing influence throughout the world. While the association of liberty and commerce was conventional in eighteenth-century thought,[19] the Americans—as former victims of what they considered an unequal, exploitative colonial system—keenly appreciated the importance of power politics in determining the terms of international trade. Thus President Ezra Stiles of Yale College predicted that the growth of "a commercial system among the maritime nations, on both sides of the Atlantick, founded on justice and reciprocity of interest, will establish the *benevolence* as well as the *opulence* of nations, and advance the progress of Society to civil perfection." Before these happy effects would be felt, however, it would be necessary to secure the equality of the United States in international trade relations, to create a "system . . . founded on justice and reciprocity."[20]

Many Americans were concerned about becoming overdependent on British manufactures and credit when trade resumed after the peace.[21] Simply giving the former mother country free access to its old colonial markets would not be in the new nation's—or the world's—best interest. Properly understood, a friendly British commentator explained, "commerce is the imports and exports of different countries for *mutual advantage*; any other commercial connections must be ruinous to one part or the other."[22] It was necessary for the United States to be "independent" economically as well as politically before it could properly benefit from international commerce—and before the world could benefit from trade with America. Therefore, a New York writer urged, Congress had to "encourage our own industry, manufactures, agriculture and commerce, by wise imposts and restrictions upon those of foreign nations." The alternative to "speedy and decisive measures" would be neo-colonial dependency: "Our citizens will not even be what they have been since the late war, the *factors* of foreign merchants; we will sink to the same state with the coasts of Africa or India, where the whole trade is in the hands of foreigners—where foreigners are everything, and the natives nothing."[23] Unless Americans were willing to abjure foreign trade altogether—and they were not, notwithstanding the counsel of republican theorists[24]—a "respectable" national government capable of protecting American interests at home and abroad was essential. A beneficial commerce depended on true reciprocity which was only possible if the new nation attained economic as well as political independence.

America presented the novel spectable of a nation dedicated to the proposition of promoting the interests of its own people. This new departure in political economy was supposed to have the most profound impact on the rest of the world and pointed toward a new, liberal world order. Americans believed that the influence of their revolution would spread through commerce and enlightenment. Commerce was supposed to be "liberalizing," in the broadest sense. Most Americans thus would not expect and would not necessarily endorse the violent overthrow of existing regimes. The liberal project which Americans saw themselves advancing was globalist and gradualist, working to expand the scope of liberty from the outside in by the transforming influence of world trade. In liberal teleology, republicanism would be the end product of the transformation of the international economy.

Constitutional reconstruction within the United States shaped these American attitudes toward world order. The ideals of 1776—the belief in the redemptive power of republican government—did not disappear, but were displaced. On one hand, natural rights claims set forth in the Declaration of Independence continued to provide the background—the underlying assumptions of American liberal internationalism. The characteristically American emphasis on the equality of states in the international community and the correlative concern with jurisdiction are grounded in naturalist principles. At the same time, American theorists projected these principles far into the future, in a vision of the good society that the spread of commerce and the enlightened pursuit of interest would ultimately create.

In the meantime, Americans sought to advance the liberal millennium by small steps—steps that depended on the effective consolidation of authority in the United States. They generally were untroubled by Utilitarian skepticism about the lawfulness of a world order without authoritative sanctions—perhaps because American practice, like that of all new nations, favored treaties over received, perhaps retrograde, and sometimes uncertain custom. Experience taught that the enforcement of treaties required the expansion of effective national power, not its supersession. Confident in their assumptions about the ultimately harmonious character of international society and in the increasing force that enlightened self-interest would give to international agreements, American diplomats and writers eagerly sought to enlarge the effective scope of positive international law. In this project they were at once naturalists and positivists. As such, they were leading proponents of the classic liberal conception of world order.

II

A more peaceful world depended on a more perfect union among states through the negotiation of treaties and the arbitration of disputes that in a less enlightened era had led to war. "The time . . . is not far distant," one American writer hoped, "when mankind shall be so far enlightened, that negociation shall render all wars unnecessary, and the uninfluenced decision of a number of uninterested powers, decide all political questions of right or wrong."[25] The willingness to negotiate—

and thus to expand the effective scope of positive international law—depended in turn on an "enlightened" recognition of the real interests of states and their citizens. American theorists suggested that international society could be rationally organized if other nations would follow their lead in adjudicating disputes and forming enlightened commercial alliances. According to Benjamin Rush, "The United States have taught the nations of the world that it is possible to terminate disputes by appeals to reason instead of the sword."[26]

America's liberalizing influence could follow one of two related paths. First, the idea of confederation or union among states could set a pattern for some form of international organization. The law of nations would govern relations among members of the union: therefore, within the boundaries of the American empire, the dreams of the great "peace planners" would be effectively implemented. Alternatively, the new nation could take an active role in rationalizing and reforming the conduct of diplomacy and extending the scope of positive international law in the unreconstructed world the planners then confronted.

Both impulses have had enduring consequences for world order and organization. Americans provided leadership and inspiration in the nineteenth-century movement for international organization and world government that set the stage for the experiments of our own era.[27] When peace activists like William Ladd advocated the creation of new institutions for making and enforcing law for the community of nations, they explicitly invoked the example of the United States. At the same time, American diplomats and jurists took the lead in expanding the range of practical applications for international law principles. Americans saw their nation as an important new source for the creation of the materials—treaties, relevant court decisions, and state practice generally—from which the working principles of international law could be deduced.

While the differences in these approaches to world order are obvious, they should not be exaggerated. The goal—a world governed by law—was the same, and neither peace planners nor proponents of international law anticipated that it would be attained easily or early. Both groups reflected a characteristic American mix of realism and optimism. In a sense, their prescriptions were symmetrical: the peace planners were "realistic" about the problem of enforcement and the effectiveness of "law" in an institutional vacuum, issues that the lawyers tended to ignore. The lawyers for their part were "realistic" about the prospects of establishing an international institutional order. They argued instead that the proliferation of agreements among states—however technically imperfect—and the expanding regime of interlocking interests in which they were grounded would inevitably produce a more orderly world.[28]

Planning for peace is always an attractive project in the aftermath of wars, especially after the Whiggish, liberal faith in the progressive development of international law has suffered a setback. But the ordinary course of diplomacy and statecraft—and the intellectual commitments and interests of diplomats, jurists, and statesmen—tend powerfully to reinforce the working assumption of the lawyers that international law and order is always "there" and capable of expansion and improvement, notwithstanding temporary reverses. This "optimism" was the leading characteristic of mainstream American thinking about world order when Henry Wheaton wrote his *Elements*.

During the same period, peace activists were busily educating public opinion on the need for more effective international organization. These two strands of thought and activity developed dialectically, one feeding on the other's failures. They each grew out of the founding era of American national history, reflecting, on one hand, the creation of a new world order in the union of states and, on the other, the institution of a central government capable of acting as an effective agent for liberty and progress in the larger world. Just as these two approaches to world order were grounded in the same original, liberal impulse, their impact on the world was ultimately convergent. Rationalization and codification of the expanding body of international legal materials led to the creation of conventions, alliances and other international organizations, however partial, temporary, or otherwise imperfect peace planners may have found them.

The peace planners were organizationalists. They looked at the creation of international law as a "constitutional" problem, questioning the authority of conventional "sources" and emphasizing the need for enforcement capabilities. But the lawyers insisted that a growing variety of "sources" flowed into the working corpus of international law: after all, there would be no such thing as international law at all if these sources were required to meet "constitutional" standards. The challenge, they argued, was to discover the principles underlying the vast, confusing array of international legal material. In committing their energies to this project, the lawyers were leaping almost as boldly into the unknown and unreal as the peace planners. To discover "order" in the materials they called international law, and thus in the society of nations that created them, depended on a priori (we argue, naturalist) assumptions as well as on a positivist determination to get the facts straight.

In an 1820 lecture to the New-York Historical Society, Wheaton made a succinct statement of the materials from which the "science" of international law could draw. Wheaton acknowledged the contributions of Wolff and Vattel but dismissed the other great treatises. Wolff deserved "the credit of separating the science from that of natural jurisprudence" while Vattel abridged Wolff's "ponderous" work "in his lively, spirited, but superficial" *Law of Nations*. These writers showed how the source material of international law could be analyzed along scientific lines. In Wheaton's view, there were no fixed and immutable principles around which commentary could be organized, with state practice simply providing illustrative examples. In fact, the relation between practice and principle was just the reverse: the sources for international law "must be sought for principally in the history of diplomatic intercourse, in the decisions of the tribunals by which the law of nations is administered, and in the ordinances of particular states." The task of the treatise writer was to "reduce that law to a written text for the direction of these tribunals, and for the information of foreign powers."[29]

Wheaton had little patience with the naturalist contention that "there is a *necessary* and *internal* law of nations, which is binding upon states as the laws of morality are binding upon individuals."[30] The "voluntary" law of nations, he maintained, had "no connexion with, or similitude to, the natural law," but was the product of progressive enlightenment. "The very relations which grow up between highly refined and civilized societies are entirely unknown in what is called a state of nature."[31]

Wheaton's conception of international law privileged contemporary sources, thus opening the door wide for significant American contributions. Americans were leading actors in a progressively more liberal world order; they had also already made important contributions to the publication, organization, and analysis of the new materials they had generated. "The science of international jurisprudence is entirely of modern structure," he asserted.[32] Its growth was directly linked to

> the great and rapid improvement in the international intercourse and policy of Europe . . . cooperating with the increasing mildness of manners in that favoured portion of the globe; and has also been promoted by the vast extension of colonization and commerce; the growing importance of pacific and neutral states [like the United States] . . . and by the salutary doctrines of political economy, teaching all nations the interest and duty of cultivating a liberal interchange of benefits by a free commercial intercourse, founded upon the basis of reciprocity.[33]

The United States was well situated to advance the international regime of law because of the widespread acceptance of the "salutary truths" of modern political economy and the enlightened character of American institutions.[34] Diplomats and jurists were conscious of their role as creators of international law. As a result, even in the first decades of national existence, "our country has not been backward in cultivating the science of which we are speaking." Such progress was possible because the distinction between moralizing theorist and amoral actor which was justified by the division between "internal" and "voluntary" law in the classic treaties was eliminated. International law was a "science" and its practitioners were scientists. For instance, Wheaton wrote:

> During the late war with Great Britain, the principles of the law of prize were ascertained and settled by those tribunals to which the administration of international law is intrusted in this country, and a great system built up, equally removed from fanciful novelties on the one side, and the extreme rigours of belligerent pretensions on the other; leaving little to be done in any future war, but to apply the general principles which have been developed to such new cases as may arise.[35]

Wheaton himself had sorted through these materials and deduced "general principles" from them in his *Digest of the Law of Maritime Captures and Prizes* (1815).[36] As occasions arose, Americans would generate further source material which would at once reflect and extend the systematic and scientific premises of their enlightened foreign policy.

Wheaton's 1820 lecture served as a prospectus for his ambitious *History of the Law of Nations* (1845), which is indeed a history of practice far more than of doctrine. It was also an argument for America's claims to assuming a leading role in the creation of a more liberal world order. In the same way, Wheaton, as a writer-diplomat intimately involved in making and codifying the new law, justified his own presumption in setting forth the working principles or *Elements* of the emerging international system. Wheaton's treatise exploited a wide range of American materials. While its form reflected the influence of the classic treatises, its substance was much more contemporary. As a treatise in international law, the *Elements* stands alone in the liberal century, but as an effort to collect, codify, and analyze legal and diplomatic materials, it was part of a flourishing American tradition.[37]

III

To assess the American impact on the liberal world order of the nineteenth and twentieth centuries, it is necessary to disentangle American and British international legal traditions. The convergence of these traditions in the later nineteenth century—part of a broader Anglo-American political and cultural rapprochement—promoted a still prevalent assumption that the liberal design combines classical political economy, Lockean naturalism, and the common law as the indivisible heritage of the English-speaking world. Articles of faith become self-fulfilling prophecies: British and American versions of liberalism are closely allied and have exercised a powerful influence on each other ever since the nineteenth century order took definite shape. A reexamination of Wheaton's *Elements* in its contemporary jurisprudential context enables us to establish the distinctive American contribution to liberal internationalism.

Beyond being liberal, the world order of the nineteenth century was strongly positivist in tenor. So, we suggest, was American constitutional thought and federal practice. The first philosophical assault on naturalism came from Hume. For the period now in question Hume's inheritors, the British Utilitarians, were the ones who gave positivism systematic attention. A flat rejection of naturalism appears in Jeremy Bentham's earliest writings: in 1776 he sharply criticized the Declaration of Independence on positivist grounds.[38] Bentham gave positivist legal theory an imperative form which dominates British jurisprudence to this day. Laws are commands; rights are fictions unless commanded. Bentham emphasized Parliament's role as lawmaker and set out to replace judge-made common law with enacted codes. This was to be the centerpiece in a program of diverse social and political reforms in the name of Utility.

While Bentham also devoted some of his boundless energy to the codification of international law, his scattered remarks on international matters lack the doctrinal coherence of his positivist liberalism applied to domestic conditions.[39] Bentham's disciple, James Mill, remedied this deficiency with remarkably vigorous and compact statements of doctrine on jurisprudence and international law that appeared in the 1820s in supplements to the *Encyclopedia Britannica*.[40] If Bentham's influence on positivist internationalism was limited by the relatively undeveloped character of his thought, no such excuse holds for Mill's lack of influence. Nevertheless, subsequent international law treatises never cite Mill. Instead they cite John Austin, whose work on jurisprudence shut the door on a systematically developed utilitarian theory of international law and world order—a door not fully reopened even in our own time.[41] Austin simply dispatched international law from the domain of law, inasmuch as sanction-bearing commands of a sovereign could not be international by definition. Utilitarians thereupon abandoned international law and order to historicalists like Sir Henry Maine and common-law naturalists who styled themselves Grotians (and who gratuitously identified American international legal thought in the same terms.)[42] British positivism and liberal internationalism suffered an artificial but permanent separation at Austin's hands. All that remained was a heightened spirit of rationalism. Thus the ideas of John Stuart Mill and Richard Cobden on intervention and the benign consequences of free trade floated on the attenuated currents of a Lockean liberalism and its ill-defined presumption of harmony of interests.[43]

Doctrinal support for American positivist internationalism came not from the Utilitarians, who are rarely even cited, but instead from the work of Emmerich de Vattel. The evidence is indisputable that Vattel's impact on diplomatic and legal practice was both far greater in the United

States than elsewhere and far greater than anyone else's.[44] Not so clear is whether Vattel was a positivist or, more importantly, whether his doctrinal position was sufficiently developed to be labeled at all.[45]

Vattel argued for the existence of two distinct types of international law, both "established by nature," but one being necessary and the other voluntary:

the former as a sacred law to be respected and obeyed by Nations and sovereigns in all their actions; the latter as a rule of conduct which the common good and welfare oblige them to accept in their mutual intercourse. The *necessary* law is derived immediately from nature; while this common mother of men merely recommends the observance of the *voluntary* law of Nations in view of the circumstances, in which Nations happen to find themselves, and for the common good.[46]

The content of the necessary law turned out to be a small number of "general laws": one holding a utilitarian standard for conduct,[47] and another establishing liberty and equality for nations: "a small republic is no less a Sovereign State than the most powerful kingdom."[48]

It can hardly be a surprise that Vattel's partition of international law into the principles necessary for a liberal-utilitarian vision of the world and positive rules from and for state practice in a working order appealed to American writers, jurists, and diplomats. What Vattel left unclear is how the voluntary law could actually be established by nature, as he alleged, if it were merely the product of formal and tacit consent by states to be bound. Such law is voluntary to the extent that states are enjoined to disregard rules whose content derogates from natural principles. In this case, however, states would no longer have consented to the rule, and it would cease to be legal anyway. Vattel fell back on a weaker position: the necessary law was "at all times obligatory on conscience," a state must always have it in mind when performing its duty; "but when there is question of what it can derive from other States, it must consult the *voluntary law*, whose rules are devoted to the welfare and advancement of universal society."[49] Inasmuch as recourse to the positive law will also disclose duties, the source of the obligation to perform one's obligations remains unclear.

Vattel is called a Grotian, at least by Grotians, because his doctrine sits half-way between naturalism and positivism.[50] In fact, he had it both ways. And so did Henry Wheaton, whose treatise of 1836 "at once attracts the attention of the whole of Europe."[51] Take Wheaton's definition of international law:

The law of nations, or international law, as understood among civilized, Christian nations, may be defined as consisting of those rules of conduct which reason deduces as consonant to justice; from the nature of the society existing among independent nations; with such definitions and modifications as may be established by general consent.[52]

Whatever we may take to be the plain meaning of these words, Wheaton did not see international law as actually being derived from natural law. A few pages earlier he said, "Without refining too much on the subject, it may properly be observed that international law is something more and other than merely natural law (the law of God) applied to the conduct of independent states considered as moral beings."[53] Wheaton went on to quote Vattel in making the case that international law cannot be derived from natural law in any strict sense (he allowed that the case may be different form individuals), so the only operative part of his definition is the last part, that is: international law consists of such definitions and modifications of rules of conduct as may be established by general consent.

If this is pure positivism, what then is the function of natural principles? It is merely to establish that, by being in a society, states are bound to consider all acts of general consent as binding—they are "moral beings capable of contracting by direct and positive consent. . . . "[54] The basis of positive action is general consent, which in the first instance is supplied in consequence of natural law. Positivists from Bentham on have invoked some version of this position to validate any positive legal order, and they have been accused of being crypto-naturalists for doing so.[55]

Like Vattel before him, Wheaton needed natural principles only to anchor the liberal premise that the working world order is made of and by states. Like the Utilitarians, Wheaton thought the order could be made to work for the collective good. He even remarked that "Grotius would, undoubtedly, have done better had he sought the origin of the natural law of Nations in the Principle of Utility . . . admitted by almost all subsequent writers as the first on international morality."[56] The other major American international legal treatise of the time was unambiguously positivist. Its author, Chancellor James Kent, castigated Wheaton for his doctrinal obscurantism.[57] But Wheaton was no obscurantist, just as Vattel was more substantial than his critics suggest. Indeed, these two men had devised a working formula for a world order both liberal and positivist.

The rise in the nineteenth century of a doctrinally indifferent positivism—one in which international law was seen simply as the aggregate of rules adduced from state practice—led to the progressive elimination of naturalist language from this working formula.[58] Because state practice did not begin in a vacuum, any more than it could be exclusively self-referring, compilations of that practice reflected organizational premises necessarily embodied in the working language of state practice. Seemingly transparent, this language was in fact affiliated with and complementary to the Vattel-Wheaton formula which, if anything, was strengthened by the abandonment of increasingly dated naturalist rhetoric.

State practice was from the very beginnings of the Western state system organized around ideas of jurisdiction inherited from Roman law.[59] The virtue of this orientation toward jurisdiction is that it is immediately reconcilable with the centrality of property in Lockean naturalism. A simple analogy might be helpful.[60] Defining legal competence, specifying conditions for the acquisition of titles, regulating intercourse across boundaries and within commons, differentiating jurisdictional consequences of war and peace—this was the main business of international law practice and doctrine from Grotius until the middle of the nineteenth century. The pattern of practice—both those crystallizing rules analogous to the Roman law and the permissive silences—honored the liberal requirements of orderly trade, free movement of capital and labor, and sheltered opportunities for development.[61] It also fostered naturalist principles in everything but name.

Because the growth of positive law is structured by these jurisdictional analogies, Grotian suppositions about right reason and human solidarity are needed neither to explain nor to insure the attractive qualities of that law from a liberal point of view. The positivist world order was an organized one, and its organization was found in jurisdictional principles and passed on in the content of rules inferred from state practice. Vattel's appeal is now easier to appreciate. He organized the law as he discerned it in state practice around established jurisdictional principles and categories. Vattel's authority was almost invariably invoked on questions of jurisdiction, the clarification of which was central to diplomacy and dispute settlement in the nineteenth century.

The anchoring of the positivist world order in a jurisdictional system compatible with the requirements of liberalism could just as well be dated from Grotius and his justly famous defense of the freedom of the high seas or from Bynkershoek's use of a rationalist-instrumentalist criterion for delimiting territorial seas (the "cannon-shot rule"). This, however, is not the Grotian tradition invoked by the Grotians. If Vattel gets the credit, it should be for his systematic but accessible presentation of the positive law of jurisdiction.[62] Wheaton's subsequent dominance as an authority stems equally from his methodical statement of state practice on matters of jurisdiction. All treatises of note thereafter are organized in much the same way. Their format, almost invariably the same, may seem today merely a matter of convention. Rather, it traces a buried history which, in its largest dimensions, is the history of the nineteenth-century world order itself—a history in which the partition of naturalist sentiments and positivist practices offers no threat to liberalism because it is accompanied by a propitious ensemble of jurisdictional ideas compatible with such sentiments and organizing such practices.

IV

American peace planners like William Ladd drew their inspiration from the same liberal-positivist schemes embedded in Wheaton's *Elements*. Because they were impatient with the gradualism of the lawyers or skeptical about upholding an international regime of law without appropriate sanctions, the peace planners proposed radically different means toward identical goals. If the positive law was already organized to meet liberal ends, simply raise the level of organization to expedite their realization; if states needed help in solving jurisdictional disputes, develop arbitral institutions to assist them; if the positive law was ambiguous because of uncertain or conflicting state practices, codify it; if states insisted on subverting rules appropriate to the liberal order, expose them to the contempt of enlightened opinion. The peace movement of the nineteenth century called for just these activities, thus revealing its essentially liberal character. The movement did not draw significantly on Continental republican or cosmopolitan traditions reflected in major peace plans from Dante to Kent. It sought not to reconstitute the world but merely to improve its already considerable capacity for order, growth, and prosperity.

The most influential scholarly treatment of the peace movement in the context of the nineteenth-century order has undoubtedly been that of F. H. Hinsley.[63] He makes no mention of Vattel in this context, nor of any naturalist strain, except for that derived from the Quaker pacifist tradition. Hinsley notes though that "Quakers had long since gone back on Penn's advocacy of international organization and now relied entirely on a religious, moral and pacifist appeal to the goodness of human nature."[64] Instead he attributes the specific program of the peace movement to Bentham and Mill because of the apparent resemblance between their models for world order and William Ladd's famous proposals. But no direct evidence of wholesale borrowing is offered. In the remainder of his discussion, Hinsley simply refers to the "Anglo-Saxon Peace Movement."[65]

We find a different interpretation in Georg Schwarzenberger's monograph on William Ladd. Here the emphasis is on Ladd's distinctive combination of optimism and realism, which "also reflected a national quality of Americans."[66] Ladd's scheme required the creation of a congress and a court of nations, with the distinctive tasks of codifying law—the functional equivalent of international legislation—and settling disputes. Indeed Ladd thought this was an original contribution.[67] That Bentham and Mill recommended a similar division of activities in a reformed world order must have escaped Ladd's attention. It certainly damages Hinsley's assertion of the dependence of Ladd on the two English writers. In Schwarzenberger's opinion, behind Ladd's scheme was the "model of the American Constitution with its strict separation of National Congress and Supreme Court."[68] Behind that, of course, lay the liberal "optimism" and positivist "realism" of Vattel and the makers of the Constitution.

If Ladd and the British Utilitarians were equally committed to the separation of legislative and judicial functions in an improved world order, they also had the same sense of what could be substituted for coercive authority in the executive sphere: public opinion. In Ladd's well-known words, public opinion was "queen of the world." Schwarzenberger remarked as he was writing in 1935 that this position was "still influential in American policy."[69] Yet there is nothing distinctively American, or Utilitarian, about this predilection. Rather, following Sheldon Wolin's argument, this position stems from the propensity in liberalism after Locke to transform conscience from an individual to a social property. This was needed to provide society with a glue once liberalism had dissolved other kinds of bonds in the name of individualism and self-interest. Given the distrust of determinate authority in the liberal tradition, the obvious solution is to let "public opinion take over where the sanctions of law cease, coercing self-regarding men to a consciousness of the interests of others."[70]

No doubt belief in the power of public opinion reached its most instrumentalist expression with Bentham's panopticon proposal, but it was an illusion "of almost all eighteenth century reformers."[71] Ladd and Bentham shared an interest in the uses of public opinion because it is the logical result of combining liberalism and positivism in the Utilitarian and organizational modes. Ladd did not need Bentham's help—Americans already thought that way. Instead, Ladd and his followers brought their ideas to Britain, where rationalism and reformism had created a receptive audience and, at least for a time, the movement flourished.

V

It is difficult to establish the precise genealogy of liberal conceptions of world order or to assess the impact of a formative period—like the American founding era—on the way those ideas were received, refined, or revised. The American contribution is obscured both by more recent doctrinal development and by emphasis on the continuing authority of the classic treatises. On one hand, the emergence of an Anglo-American international legal "tradition" in the late nineteenth century has exaggerated the putative influence of British Utilitarian positivism: liberal internationalism has thus been submerged in the history of domestic liberalism. On the other, Grotius, Pufendorf, and the other great masters of international law are presumed to have staked out the doctrinal positions within which their nineteenth-century successors worked.

A reexamination of the works of Henry Wheaton enables us to rehabilitate a crucial and neglected era in the development of international law and to better appreciate the specifically liberal character of emerging conceptions of world order. Wheaton and like-minded writers and jurists adapted Vattelian premises to the rapidly expanding scope of international diplomatic and commercial relations. Their "constitutional positivism," to borrow Robert Cover's apt phrase, helped imprint a distinctively American character on the new world order.[72]

The radically different prescriptions of organizationalists like William Ladd were grounded in the same complex of liberal values and goals. Lawyers and peace planners alike sought peace and prosperity in an international regime of law. Differences over the best means to achieve world order reflected the ambiguous legacy of America's founding fathers. As lawyers and "realists," the founders hoped that the example and influence of republican diplomacy would inaugurate a more rational, enlightened, and orderly epoch in international history. As constitutional reformers, they were convinced that the preservation of peace among the American states depended on the organization of effective authority under a national government.

Subsequent generations of theorists and practitioners could draw on either the "legal-diplomatic" or "organizational" strands in American constitutionalism—or on both. Indeed, the tendency for these apparently distinct approaches to world order to converge—for instance, in movements to codify international law or to create arbitral commissions, tribunals, and other international organizations—demonstrates best their common liberal origins.

NOTES

The authors are grateful to R. Kent Newmeyer of the University of Connecticut and Alfred Rubin of the Fletcher School, Tufts University, for instructive readings.

1. Henry Wheaton, *Elements of International Law* (Philadelphia, 1836). The eighth edition of 1866 (rev. by Richard Henry Dana, Jr.) became the only English language treatise reprinted in the famous Carnegie series of *Classics of International Law*, George Grafton Wilson, ed. (Oxford: Oxford University Press, 1936). On Wheaton's career see Elizabeth Feaster Baker, *Henry Wheaton* (Philadelphia: University of Pennsylvania Press, 1936).

2. Robert R. Palmer, *The Age of the Democratic Revolution*, 2 vols. (Princeton, N.J.: Princeton University Press, 1959–64); Carl J. Friedrich, *The Impact of American Constitutionalism Abroad* (Boston: Boston University Press, 1967); Richard B.

Morris, *The Emerging Nations and the American Revolution* (New York: Harper & Row, 1970); and *The Impact of the American Revolution Abroad* (Washington, D.C.: Library of Congress, 1976). For case studies of the reception of American constitutional ideas see Durand Echeverria, *Mirage in the West: A History of the French Image of American Society to 1815* (Princeton, N.J.: Princeton University Press, 1957); Horst Dippel, *Germany and the American Revolution, 1770–1800*, trans. Bernhard Uhlendorf (Chapel Hill: University of North Carolina Press, 1977); and Colin Bonwick, *English Radicals and the American Revolution* (Durham, N.C.: Duke University Press, 1977).

3. See the discussions of Edward Handler, *America and Europe in the Political Thought of John Adams* (Cambridge, Mass.: Harvard University Press, 1964); and Louis Hartz, *The Liberal Tradition in America* (New York: Harcourt Brace, 1955), 3–78.

4. Adam Smith, *An Inquiry into the Nature and Causes of the Wealth of Nations* (London, 1776), Book Four, Chap. VIII ("Of Colonies").

5. Charles William (Earl Fitzwilliam) and Sir Richard Bourke, eds., *The Works and Correspondence of the Right Honourable Edmund Burke*, vols. 1–2, *Correspondence, 1744–1797*, 2nd ed. (London, 1852), 2:435. For a discussion of Burke as one of the founding fathers of Anglo-American liberalism see Robert Kelley, *The Transatlantic Persuasion: The Liberal-Democratic Mind in the Age of Gladstone* (New York: Alfred A. Knopf, 1969), 80–100.

6. Extract from *Liverpool Advertiser*, reprinted in *Independent Chronicle* (Boston), Nov. 24, 1785.

7. On the importance of commercial alliances see Felix Gilbert, *To the Farewell Address: Ideas of Early American Foreign Policy* (Princeton, N.J.: Princeton University Press, 1961), 44–75. But also see James H. Hutson, *John Adams and the Diplomacy of the American Revolution* (Lexington: University of Kentucky Press, 1980), who correctly emphasizes the centrality of the balance of power and interest of state in American thinking about international relations. This "realism" was not incompatible with liberal premises: as Hutson notes, 10, "Americans genuinely believed that [the balance of power] was a progressive principle in international affairs." We are also indebted to Gerald Stourzh's excellent *Benjamin Franklin and American Foreign Policy* 2nd ed. (Chicago: University of Chicago Press, 1969).

8. Albert K. Weinberg, *Manifest Destiny: A Study of Nationalist Expansionism in American History* (Baltimore, Md.: Johns Hopkins University Press, 1935), chap. 1, shows how natural rights arguments could be deployed for practical effect.

9. Franklin to Ferdinand Grand, Oct. 22, 1787, *Documentary History of the Constitution of the United States* 5 vols. (Washington, D.C.: Government Printing Office, 1901–5), 4:341–42. For Franklin's attitude toward international law see Stourzh, *Benjamin Franklin*, 227–31. See also Robert R. Livingston to Lafayette, Jan. 10, 1783, Julian P. Boyd and Robert J. Taylor, eds., *The Susquehannah Company Papers* 11 vols. (Wilkes-Barre, Penn. and Ithaca, N.Y.: Wyoming Historical and Geological Society and Cornell University Press, 1962–71) 7:252, for the claim that the congressional court in *Connecticut* v. *Pennsylvania* (1782) had successfully put the law of nations into operation. On the early American state system in practice see Peter S. Onuf, *The Origins of the Federal Republic: Jurisdic-*

tional Controversies in the United States, 1775–1787 (Philadelphia: University of Pennsylvania Press, 1983), esp. chap. 1.

10. [Madison], "Universal Peace," Philadelphia, Jan. 31, 1792, *National Gazette,* Feb. 2, 1792.

11. "Philodemus," *New York Gazetteer,* March 22, 1785.

12. Quoted in Stourzh, *Benjamin Franklin,* 229.

13. Price, *Observations on the Importance of the American Revolution, and the Means of Making it a Benefit to the World* (London, 1785 ed.), reprinted in Bernard Peach, ed., *Richard Price and the Ethical Foundations of the American Revolution* (Durham, N.C.: Duke University Press, 1979), 177–224, quotation at 187.

14. Price to Benjamin Rush, June 26, 1783, ibid. 320–21.

15. These reports are surveyed in Leon Fraser, *English Opinion of the American Constitution and Government (1783–1798)* (New York: Columbia University Press, 1915), 31–43 and passim.

16. Letter from M. Turgot, in Price, *Observations,* 215–24, quotation at 222.

17. Onuf, *Origins of the Federal Republic,* 173–85; and Frederick W. Marks III, *Independence on Trial: Foreign Affairs and the Making of the Constitution* (Baton Rouge: Louisiana State University Press, 1973).

18. T[homas] Pownall, *A Memorial Addressed to the Sovereigns of America* (London, 1783), 129.

19. See the stimulating discussions in Albert O. Hirschman, *The Passions and the Interests: Political Arguments for Capitalism Before its Triumph* (Princeton, N.J.: Princeton University Press, 1977); and in Ralph Lerner, "Commerce and Character: The Anglo-American as a New-Model Man," *William and Mary Quarterly,* 3rd ser., 26 (1979): 3–26.

20. Ezra Stiles, *The United States Elevated to Glory and Honor* (1783 Connecticut election sermon), 2nd ed. (Worcester, Mass., 1785), 49–50. See also William Vans Murray, "Political Sketches" (written in 1784–85), *American Museum* II (September 1787): 241–43.

21. For example, "Common Sense," New York, Dec. 2, 1783, *Virginia Gazette* (Richmond), Jan. 3, 1784; "Brutus," *Gazette of the State of Georgia* (Savannah), Sept. 30, 1784; Memorial of the Committee of Merchants, Philadelphia, April 6, 1785, *Virginia Journal* (Alexandria), June 16, 1785; [St. George Tucker], *Reflections on the Policy and Necessity of Encouraging the Commerce . . . of the United States* (New York, 1786), 14 and passim.

22. "Candidus," *London Evening Post,* n.d. given, reprinted in *Pennsylvania Gazette* (Philadelphia), July 21, 1784.

23. Extract of a letter, New York, March 14, 1785, *Independent Chronicle,* April 14, 1785.

24. Richard Price, *Observations,* 210; translation of a letter from M. Target, Paris, Oct. 24, 1783, *Gazette of Georgia,* Sept. 23, 1784; and Count de Mirabeau, *Reflections on [Price's] Observations on the Importance of the American Revolution* (Philadelphia, 1786), 11–13. But see Thomas Jefferson to George Washington, March 15, 1784, and to G. K. van Hogendorp, Oct. 13, 1785, Julian Boyd et al., eds., *The Papers of Thomas Jefferson,* 22 vols. to date (Princeton, N.J.: Princeton University Press, 1950-), 7:25–27, 8:631–34.

25. A letter from Baltimore to a gentleman in Philadelphia, March 15, 1785, *Freeman's Journal* (Philadelphia), March 23, 1785.

26. Benjamin Rush [to Elias Boudinot], "Observations on the Federal Procession," Philadelphia, July 9, 1788, *American Museum* 4 (July 1788): 75–78, reprinted in Lyman Butterfield, ed., *The Letters of Benjamin Rush*, 2 vols. (Princeton, N.J.: Princeton University Press, 1951), 1:473.

27. Merle Curti, *Peace or War: The American Struggle: 1636–1936* (New York: W.W. Norton, 1936), 16–46.

28. The "lawyers" approach is apparent in Wheaton's works, discussed below. For an interesting example of American naturalist skepticism about international law reflecting contemporary hostility to the common law [both "bear the marks of feudality and ignorance"], see William John Duane, *The Law of Nations, investigated in a popular manner. Addressed to the farmers of the United States* (Philadelphia, 1809), quotation at 6. Advocating a "confederation of nations for protecting weak states," Duane emphasizes that treaties "have been the basis of association among nations" and that their proliferation had already normalized and liberalized international relations by creating alliances or partial confederations (102). The argument finally is virtually indistinguishable from the lawyers' brief for treaties as a privileged source for international law. For an earlier attack on the traditional law of nations see Joel Barlow, *A Letter Addressed to the People of Piedmont* (New York, 1795), 41–43, in which the author promotes (1) republican revolutions and (2) the example of the United States as an international organization for resolving controversies among states.

29. Wheaton, "An Anniversary Discourse, Delivered Before the New-York Historical Society, Dec. 28, 1820," *Collections of the New-York Historical Society* 3 (New York, 1821): 281–320, quotation at 314–15.

30. Ibid., 294–95.

31. Ibid., 297.

32. Ibid., 292.

33. Ibid., 316.

34. Ibid., 291.

35. Ibid., 314–15n. Among the important American contributions, Wheaton cites James Madison's *An Examination of the British Doctrine, which subjects to capture a Neutral Trade, Not Open in the Time of Peace* (Washington, 1806), reprinted in Gaillard Hunt, ed., *The Writings of James Madison*, 9 vols. (New York: G.P. Putnam, 1900–10), 7:204–375. Madison includes an interesting discussion of international law sources (listed 208) in which he discounts the importance of existing treatises, concluding "that all further meliorations of the code of public law, are to be expected" from treaties (240).

36. For an appreciation of Wheaton's *Digest*, with an argument for the importance of law and lawyers in American society and a prediction that American writers would excel "in the department of jurisprudence," see [Richard Rush], *American Jurisprudence . . . being a few reflections suggested on reading "Wheaton on Captures"* (Washington, 1815), 6–7 and passim.

37. See, for instance, Jonathan Eliot, *Diplomatic Code of the United States: embracing a collection of treaties and conventions between the United States and foreign powers, from the year 1778–1827. With an index to the principal cases decided in the courts of the United States, upon points connected with their foreign relations. . . .* (Washington, 1827).

38. He later became an advocate of democracy as practiced in the United

States. H. L. A. Hart, *Essay on Bentham* (Oxford: Oxford University Press, 1982), 53–78.

39. Mark W. Janis, "Jeremy Bentham and the Fashioning of 'International Law'," *American Journal of International Law* 78 (1984): 418–26. His first, long unpublished work on international law exposed naturalist premises in Blackstone's treatment of international law in the *Commentaries*.

40. Privately printed as *Essays on Government, Jurisprudence, Liberty of the Press and the Law of Nations* (London, 1825), and apparently not reprinted until 1967.

41. H. L. A. Hart's *The Concept of Law* (Oxford: Oxford University Press, 1961) opens the door for legal theory generally; his treatment of international law as law by analogy, familiar as it is vacuous, does not.

42. L. Oppenheim, *International Law* (London, 2nd ed., 1912), 1:92, 98; Hersch Lauterpacht, "The Grotian Tradition in International Law," in Eli Lauterpacht, ed., *International Law, Being the Collected Papers of Hersch Lauterpacht* (Cambridge, 1875), 2:307–65. For a critical, comparative treatment of Grotius and the Grotians, see Hedley Bull, "The Grotian Conception of International Society," in Herbert Butterfield and Martin Wright, eds., *Diplomatic Investigations* (Cambridge, Mass.: Harvard University Press, 1968), 51–73. Edward H. Carr's influential assertion that Benthamite rationalism transplanted to the United States became the "utopian background" for the League of Nations is undocumented and, given the general sway of rationalism in the liberal order, unnecessary. *The Twenty Years' Crisis, 1919–1939* (New York: Harper & Row, rev. ed., 1946), 22–26.

43. Hedley Bull, *The Anarchical Society* (New York: Columbia University Press, 1977), 251–52.

44. Albert de Lapradelle, "Introduction," in Emmerich de Vattel, *The Law of Nations or the Principles of Natural Law Applied to the Conduct and to the Affairs of Nations and Sovereigns*, vol. 3 of *Classics of International Law* (Washington, D.C.: Carnegie Institution, 1916), xxvii-xxxiii; Frances Stephen Ruddy, *International Law in the Enlightenment* (Dobbs Ferry, N.Y.: Oceana, 1975), 281–85 and citations therein; and Daniel George Lang, *Foreign Policy and the Early Republic* (Baton Rouge: Louisiana University Press, 1985), 13–33.

45. See Vattel, *Law of Nations*, xlii-xlv, for a sample of highly critical judgments, not the least of which was Bentham's, but none of which (by happenstance?) were American. Even de Lapradelle's friendly voice intones: "what Vattel lacks is a legal philosophy," liii.

46. Ibid., 11a.

47. "The first general law . . . is that each Nation should contribute as far as it can to the happiness and advancement of other nations. But as its duties toward itself clearly prevail over its duties towards others, a Nation owes to itself, as a prime consideration, whatever it can do for its own happiness and advancement." Ibid., 5.

48. Ibid., 7.

49. Ibid., 9. Emphasis in original.

50. Oppenheim, *International Law*, 92.

51. Ibid., 98.

52. Wheaton, *Elements of International Law* (1836 ed.), 46.

53. Ibid., 42.

54. Ibid., 43. This and the preceding passage, which we take to be crucial to understanding Wheaton's doctrine, was deleted from the 1866 edition and replaced with summaries of Wolff's (see below) and Vattel's doctrinal stances. Wheaton, *Elements of International Law* (8th ed., 1866), 11–15.

55. This accusation is made both by Grotians who find the natural order in positive law and by latter-day scientific positivists who are amused to find "trans-empirical" values in a frame of reference ostensibly concerned only with legal facts. See for respective examples, Lauterpacht, op. cit., 330–32; and Myres S. McDougal, Harold D. Lasswell and W. Michael Reisman, "Theories about International Law: Prologue to a Configurative Jurisprudence," *Virginia Journal of International Law* 8 (1968): 253–58.

56. Wheaton, *Elements of International Law* (8th ed., 1866), 7, citing Bentham. This passage is not to be found in the 1836 ed. Note Carr's apt remark that " 'the greatest happiness of the greatest number' was the nineteenth century definition of the content of natural law," Carr, *Twenty Years' Crisis*, 23.

57. J. T. Abdy, *Kent's Commentary on International Law* (Cambridge, 1866), 4–6. First published in 1826 as Part I, Volume I of Kent's *Commentaries on American Law*.

58. The first positivist in this mold is probably Cornelius Van Bynkershoek, writing in the early decades of the eighteenth century. The dominant figures in the last half of the century are Johan Jacob Moser and Georg Friedrich von Martens. The triumph of the Napoleonic Code reinforced empirically oriented positivism as a Continental preference, while doctrinal indifference prevented serious clashes with Utilitarian positivism. Meanwhile the rise of scientific positivism in the nineteenth century strengthened their shared concern for the facts of the law.

59. Charles Howard McIlwain, *Constitutionalism: Ancient and Modern* (Ithaca, N.Y.: Cornell University Press, rev. ed., 1947), chap. 3, argued the same for the domestic legal orders of Western states.

60. On the analogy with Roman law, see Hersch Lauterpacht, "Private Law Sources and Analogies in International Law," in Lauterpacht, ed., *Collected Papers of Lauterpacht*, 184–88. Lauterpacht's review of major writers fails to include Vattel or note the Lockean connection.

61. We prefer "silences" to "gaps," in view of the extensive debate over whether a system of laws logically can have gaps, as opposed to a blanket permissive rule: that which is not proscribed is permitted. See, e.g., Hersch Lauterpacht, "Some Observations on the Prohibition of '*Non Liquet*' and the Completeness of the Law," in ibid., 213–37.

62. Note that Christian Wolff, whose guidance Vattel readily recognized, produced the first such systematic treatise. Wolff's influence was limited both by the demands of his presentation and the dependence of his system on the idea of a "great republic (*Civites Maxima*) set up by nature herself of which all the Nations of the world are members." Positive international law is "the civil law of this great republic." Vattel, whose words these are (*Law of Nations*, 9a), observed that Wolff's position failed to satisfy him because "the fiction of such a republic is neither reasonable nor well enough founded to deduce therefrom the rules of a Law of Nations. . . . " Evidently Vattel's liberal audience agreed. See also Ruddy, *International Law in the Enlightenment*, 65–77, 97–110, 306–30.

63. F. H. Hinsley, *Power and the Pursuit of Peace* (Cambridge, England: Cambridge University Press, 1963).

64. Ibid., 93.

65. Ibid., 101.

66. Georg Schwarzenberger, *William Ladd: An Examination of an American Proposal for an International Tribunal* (London: Stevens, 1935), 25.

67. Ibid., 18.

68. Ibid., 25, with citations from Ladd and his follower Elihu Burritt.

69. Ibid., 74; see also Carr, *Twenty Years' Crisis*, 31–36.

70. Sheldon Wolin, *Politics and Vision* (Boston, Mass.: Little, Brown, 1960), 348.

71. Michel Foucault, "The Eye of Power," in *Power/Knowledge* (New York: Pantheon, 1980), 161. Foucault felt that the panopticon proposal, which sought to organize penal control through detached supervision, presages the organization of social control through public media as a dominant feature of liberalism thereafter.

72. Robert Cover, *Justice Accused* (New Haven, Conn.: Yale University Press, 1975), 25–28. Cover identifies "constitutional positivism" as Blackstone's ambiguous legacy to United States constitutional thought and practice.

4

The Influence of American Constitutionalism in Postwar Europe:

THE BONN REPUBLIC BASIC LAW AND THE CONSTITUTION OF THE FIFTH FRENCH REPUBLIC

William Safran

William Safran has prepared a "posthole" study comparing the parallels between two European constitutions—that of West Germany in 1949 and France in 1958—with American constitutionalism. Cognizant of the great differences in the historical development of the three countries, Safran finds, nevertheless, certain intriguing resemblances. The reasons for the development of these parallels, however, were quite dissimilar. In the case of West Germany, there had been evidence of American influence in the past—in the Frankfurt Constitution of 1848–49 and the Weimar Constitution of 1919—but the fact that the United States had been an occupying power in the post–World War II period played, perhaps, an even greater role in the formulation of the Bonn Constitution of 1949. As far as France was concerned, the Americans and French had had a symbiotic relationship in regard to certain constitutional doctrines stretching back to the ideas and ideals of the European Enlightenment, the constitutions written during the French and American revolutions, and subsequent French constitutional formulations thereafter.

At a time when Americans are marking the two-hundredth anniversary of the framing of the United States Constitution, they are bound to reflect not only on the success of this instrument but also on its influence abroad. This essay focuses on the influence of American constitutionalism on France and West Germany because some of their constitutional doctrines and several provisions of their current constitutions show an intriguing resemblance to those of the United States.

It is reasonable to attribute a number of developments in Western Europe in general, and in France and West Germany in particular, to American influence: the strengthening of the democratic ethos, the growth of technocracy, the diffusion of mass culture, the pattern of educational reforms, the intermittent fascination with market liberalism, and the widespread use of the English language. However, it is not always easy to "prove" that this or that constitutional feature was imported from the United States. One of the obstacles to an unambiguous grafting of American features onto French and German constitutional documents was their divergent historical development. Royal absolutism, statism, and a well-entrenched administrative tradition in both countries made it difficult for American notions of limited government to strike firm roots; class differences, themselves vestiges of a feudal tradition, were reflected in differences in constitutional values; and wars, economic disasters, and social dislocations sometimes led to a search for an extra-constitutional "savior." Secondly, some of the French and German constitutional ideas that resemble American ones were based on common intellectual sources that also inspired the founding fathers. Thirdly, national pride and public opinion often made it difficult to constituent elites in France and Germany to adopt American provisions or to admit any imitation. Finally, the American influence on both the West German and French post–World War II constitutions has been limited by a kind of ideological diachronism. Thus, during the nineteenth century, the influence of American political doctrines was diluted by the weakness of liberalism on the continent—a weakness attested to by the fate of the constitutions of 1848 in France and Germany. Although after World War II both countries were much more receptive to American *political* liberalism, this receptivity was modified by other major ideologies that were weak in the United States but strong on the European continent: socialism and Catholicism. Both of these ideologies were embodied in socioeconomic (i.e., welfare state) provisions that endowed the postwar West German, French (Fourth Republic), and several other Western European constitutions with "programmatic" qualities, in sharp contrast to the "mechanistic" nature of the American Constitution, which in its specific articles was concerned largely with the relationship between institutions and the distribution of functions among power holders.[1]

THE FIFTH REPUBLIC: ANALOGIES AND COMPARISONS

Legacies and Problems of Earlier Regimes

All French republics, from the First to the Fifth, claim to have been inspired by the Revolution of 1789. The fact that some of the conceptions prevalent at the time were found also in the newly established United States has led a number of commentators, including Frenchmen, to suggest a direct American influence. Others have argued that French constitution-makers never understood American principles very well; that it was, under prevailing conditions, difficult to transship ideas across the oceans with sufficient speed; and that whatever American ideas ultimately reached France were based anyway on original French ones that had been vulgarized by the Americans. Still others took a middle position: that influences were reciprocal and that both countries learned from one another.

The common fund of political ideas and their bearing on the French constitutional development after the Revolution of 1789—specifically, the constitutions of 1791 and 1848—are dealt with elsewhere in this volume. One point that needs to be stressed here is that in the twentieth century—in the waning years of the Third Republic (a regime that lasted from 1870 to 1940) and throughout the Fourth Republic (1946–58), both systems embodying classic parliamentary patterns—many French scholars and politicians deplored the weakness of the French executive and admired the strength of the American president. Few critics, however, were willing to look to the American Constitution as a guide for determining the position of the president (beyond the idea of a popular election). Although many of the French accepted the principle of the separation of powers, they considered that principle to be best anchored, in practice, in an independent judiciary and/or in a clear assignment of tasks among various parts of the state rather than a disjunction of executive and legislative responsibilities that might lead to a decision-making paralysis.

After World War I, many potential reformers were hesitant to adopt the checks-and-balances approach of the United States when they noted Woodrow Wilson's failure in 1919 to obtain congressional approval of the Treaty of Versailles.[2] Still others hesitated to use the American presidency as a model for the opposite reason: its great strength vis-à-vis the legislature. They felt that such strength, while moderated in the United States by federalism, would lead to a despotic executive in highly centralized France.[3] Therefore, what remained of use in the American presidency was the provision for direct popular elections, a feature ultimately adopted in the Fifth Republic.[4]

Popular Sovereignty and Effective Government

The Fifth French Republic Constitution contains a number of features that are so comparable to the American Constitution as to suggest that its drafters were influenced by the American experience or—at the least—had studied that experience. The very process of drafting the new constitution paralleled that of the American Constitution in two ways:

the absence, in 1958, of a directly elected constituent assembly (*pouvoir constituant*), an absence that was a clear departure from the French tradition of republican constitution-making; and the avoidance of any glare of publicity.[5] The members of the Constitutional Consultative Committee of 1958 referred to the American Constitution as, indeed, they referred to other foreign constitutions.[6] But Michel Debré, one of the "parents" of the Fifth Republic Constitution, nowhere suggested that the committee leaned significantly on the American model. Debré admitted, however, that the committee members adhered to at least some features found in the American Constitution: (1) the provision for a chief of state "worthy of the name" who would be able to have his own mandate and assume his own responsibilities; (2) a parliamentary election method "as close as possible to the British American system, the one used by the first French republicans—election by majority vote"; and (3) a Constitutional Council that would assure the constitutionality of institutional-jurisdictional relationships.[7]

However, if these features resembled those of the American Constitution, the resemblance was due in large part to the fact that the Consultative Committee leaned upon earlier French constitutional models—such as those of 1791 and November 1848—that had been, perhaps, more directly inspired by the American example or at least by a set of theories that had, more or less simultaneously, inspired the founding fathers. Debré was careful to point out that the American Constitution could not have been copied by the writers of the Fifth Republic Constitution, because they operated under different circumstances. Whereas the former was written to prevent a continuation of the kind of centralized and arbitrary government that had characterized British colonial rule, the latter was written to prevent the continuation of the weak and unstable rule associated with parliamentary predominance. Moreover, General Charles de Gaulle, the other "parent" of the Fifth Republic Constitution, probably harbored too much resentment against the Anglo-Americans to be much influenced by their constitutions, or, at any rate, to acknowledge such influence publicly.[8]

During World War II, Debré, while discussing the sort of republic France should set up after Liberation, had opposed the American presidential model because a strong executive was too dangerous in view of the periodic inclination of the French toward a "man on horseback." Moreover, after their experience with Marshal Philippe Pétain as the Chief of State of the Vichy puppet regime, the French feared a strong executive on the grounds that he might become a dictator. Later, after the postwar experience of ineffective government, Debré changed his mind and expressed a preference for the American type of presidential system, largely because it concentrated power unambiguously.[9]

There are some examples of phraseology in the Fifth Republic Constitution that look as if they might have been copied straight from American sources. Thus Article 2, which proclaims that the principle of the Constitution is "government of the people, by the people, and for the people," seems to have been taken verbatim from Lincoln's Gettysburg Address.[10] Similarly, Article 89, which asserts that "the republican form of government shall not be subject to amendment," reminds one of American constitutionalism.[11] When one deals with specific institutional features and relationships, however, one is much less certain about the direct American influence. What appear to be American parallels may in fact be purely French precedents or may have been effectively de-Americanized through French adaptation and interpretation.

Separation of Powers

A case in point is the notion of separation of powers. In his Bayeux speech of 1946 (as on other occasions during the Fourth Republic) General de Gaulle expressed himself as follows: "Both experience and principle require the public powers—legislative, executive, judicial—should be clearly separated and strongly balanced."[12] In the same speech, he declared that the executive should not be drawn from the legislature, for that would lead to an excessive identification of cabinet members with the parliament and result in a confusion, and perhaps dilution, of power. It has been pointed out[13] that various meanings can be attached to the concept of separation of powers, and that there exist three major views concerning it: (1) the continental view, which envisions a separation of agencies, functions, and persons; (2) the view of the American founding fathers, who wanted a partial separation of powers, i.e., the "pure" doctrine modified by the notion of checks and balances; and (3) a view commonly held in Britain, i.e., judicial independence vis-à-vis the legislature and/or the government.[14] A pure separation of powers, implying a complete separation of institutions, functions, and roles, exists nowhere, and a partial separation, implying *some* division of labor and some aspect of checks and balances, exists in all industrialized democracies.

The Fifth Republic combines Montesquieu's ideas of a division of labor—what would nowadays be called "functional differentiation"—with Alexis de Tocqueville's ideas of popular sovereignty, executive responsibility, and the separate origins and appointments ("elite recruitment") of the president and the parliament.[15] According to one (British) interpretation, Article 23 of the Fifth Republic Constitution, which forbids the concurrent holding of national executive and parliamentary positions, should be construed as "separation of powers on the model of the Constitution of the United States," which provides (Article 1, Sec. 6) that "no person holding any office under the United States shall be a member of either House during his continuance in office."[16] According to another view,[17] the French reinterpreted separation of powers to mean not a separation between executive and legislature, but rather between government and bureaucracy or between politics and administration (a Weberian distinction).[18] But the first interpretation is vitiated by the fact (clearly anchored in the French Constitution) that government bills have priority and that cabinet members participate actively in the legislative process, including debates. The second interpretation must be challenged on the ground that de Gaulle drew many cabinet members from the civil service and that throughout the Fifth Republic, civil servants have effectively "colonized" the legislature. Finally, the idea of checks and balances was undermined (at least between 1958 and 1986) by the institutional weaknesses of the Parliament.

It might even be argued that until 1986 there was less separation of powers in the Fifth than there was in the Fourth Republic. In the Constitution of the latter, there was a provision (Article 13) that stipulated that "the National Assembly shall vote the laws. It may not delegate this right," which was rather similar to the American constitutional provision (Article 1, Sec. 1) declaring that "all legislative powers herein granted shall be vested in a Congress." It may be suggested, of course, that the Fourth Republic provision was merely an expression of discomfort about an excessive resort to delegated legislation (i.e., rule by decree). In any case, the Fifth Republic Constitution abandoned even that symbolic move in the direction of separation of powers when it distributed rule-initiating and rule-making powers to the government (Articles 36–39), the president (Article 16), and the people (referendum, Articles 3, 11, and 89).

The Position of the President

There is a certain analogy between the olympian position of the Fifth Republic president and the American president. Both are elected by popular vote (in the United States, de facto, and in France, with the constitutional amendment of 1962), and both have powers of appointment and pardon. Both are viewed as guardians of the constitution. Articles 5 and 16 provide that the French president "shall see to it that the constitution is respected," shall protect the independence of the nation, and "shall insure, by his *arbitrage* ('arbitrament'), the regular functioning of the public authorities [and] the continuity of the state." These articles are somewhat stronger variants of the American president's oath of office (Article 2, Sec. 1) and Article 2, Sec. 3, which stipulates that "he shall take care that the laws be faithfully executed." Moreover, just as in the United States the idea of the stewardship role of the president—going beyond his specific decision-making responsibilities—had been elaborated upon by Washington, Lincoln, Wilson, and the two Roosevelts, so President de Gaulle and, after March 6, 1986, President François Mitterand emphasized the presidential office as a "bully pulpit." Similarly, the French president's preeminence in foreign affairs resembles that of the American president in that it derives more clearly from the power of sovereignty than from a specific constitutional enabling article.[19]

But these provisions could also be construed as a throwback to monarchism, or rather, a particular interpretation of the role of the monarch. According to Nicholas Wahl, the idea of presidential *arbitrage* could be considered a modern republican restatement of the "federative" powers of the British king, as originally discussed by John Locke in his *Second Treatise of Civil Government*: a chief of state above parties, who represents the unity of the nation, deals with other countries, and intervenes (if necessary against either the "government" or the legislature) when circumstances so require.[20] In practice, of course, the suprapartisan character of the American and the French Fifth Republic president has been equally modified, as both are clearly identified with a political party during and after their election.

Judicial Review

There is reason to believe that the establishment in 1958 of the Constitutional Council (*Conseil constitutionnel*) and (beginning in the early 1970s) the increasing practice by that body of nullifying legislation judged unconstitutional were influenced by American precedent. However, in this case, too, French precedents should not be ignored. Antecedents to the Constitutional Council can be found in the Constitution of the Year VIII (1799), the Constitution of 1852, and the Constitution of 1946 (the "Constitutional Committee").[21] But the first constitution did not last long, and the second was perverted by Louis Napoleon's imperial autocracy. The Fourth Republic, moreover, like the Third after the resignation of President Patrice de Mac-Mahon (1879), had been so fully committed to parliamentary supremacy that judicial invalidation of legislative acts could not be accepted. The activities of the Constitutional Council do resemble those of the United States Supreme Court in that it has been deciding jurisdictional conflicts and (since the early 1970s) has acted as a guardian of civil liberties. However, whereas the arbitration of the Supreme Court has occasionally related to the division of power between the federal government and the states, that of the Constitutional Council has concerned itself most frequently with "the fragmentation of lawmaking between executive and Parliament,"[22] and not between the national and subnational authorities.

The power to nullify parliamentary acts (or rather bills before their promulgation) is no more explicitly stated in the Fifth Republic Constitution than it is in the American. It is quite possible (but not provable) that the Council, in arrogating to itself the right to void legislation, was inspired by the precedent of *Marbury v. Madison.*[23] However, there remain important differences between the Council and the United States Supreme Court. The Council does not judge "cases and controversies" arising from legislation already on the statute books, and matters can be referred to it only by official agents of the state, such as the government, senators, or deputies, rather than by private citizens (as in the West German "constitutional complaint") or at its own discretion (as in the American writ of certiorari). Thus, a French citizen cannot appeal a violation of constitutional provisions if both the executive and the legislative branches refuse to challenge the violation. Moreover, the Council has certain functions not possessed by the United States Supreme Court, among them the certification of presidential election results, the supervision (and, if necessary, nullification) of parliamentary elections and referenda, and the determination of presidential incapacity (a subject left in the United States to the Congress). Finally, the Council members (unlike Anglo-American high court judges who have life tenure) are appointed, in typical continental fashion, for a specified number of years. Nevertheless, it should be noted that Council members do not reflect the views of the president any more clearly than do Supreme Court members—at least initially—since the French president appoints only one third of them, the other two-thirds being chosen by the speakers of the two chambers of parliament. In 1982 the Constitutional Council voided parts of a government bill designed to nationalize selected industries, on the grounds that the compensation offered to private shareholders was too low and therefore represented an unconstitutional deprivation of property. In this case, the Council behaved much like the United States Supreme Court during the early New Deal period and was accused by the Socialist government of unwarranted meddling.

Miscellaneous Features

There is an interesting interpretive or practical parallel—it amounts almost to convergence—between the American and French republican constitutional traditions. Neither the Third Republic Constitution nor the American Constitution (until the ratification of the Twenty-second Amendment) contained any restriction on the right of a president to run for reelection indefinitely. However, in both countries it became accepted practice that presidential terms be limited—in France to one seven-year term, and in the United States to two four-year terms. We know that Franklin D. Roosevelt's violation of that tradition led to the Twenty-second Amendment. We might assume that the violation of the one-term pattern by Albert Lebrun, who was elected to a second term in 1939—the reason being, by analogy to Roosevelt's reelection to a third term in 1940, that the country was in the midst of war—would have led to a similar formal limitation if the Third Republic had survived.[24] It is true that in the Fifth Republic there is no one-term limit. But such a limit—or the reduction of the presidential term of office to five or six years—has been proposed on several occasions, most recently by former president Valéry Giscard d'Estaing.[25] Moreover, it can be argued that both the French electorate's lack of enthusiasm for de Gaulle's serving out his second term and its failure to reelect Giscard can be attributed to the same kind of tendency: that is, not to countenance any excessively long presidential incumbency as has existed in the United States.[26]

Another comparison may be made between the positions of the American vice president and the Fifth Republic premier. Constitutionally, of course, the two positions are quite different, and no French political scientist or statesman would publicly suggest that the premier was intended to be a kind of American vice president. Yet the parallels are striking: In both cases, the incumbents have been (in the United States, since the ratification of the Twelfth Amendment in 1804, and in France, at least until 1986) selected by the presidents, who have defined many of the actual responsibilities of the vice president or premier. Both the vice president and the premier have looked upon their positions as preparing them for eventual succession to the presidency (though in the United States this situation developed more markedly after World War II). It should be kept in mind that at least five premiers thus far have expressed their presidential ambitions,[27] and that premiers, like vice presidents, have tried to proclaim their loyalty and usefulness to the president and at the same time to distance themselves from him and build their own power bases.

One French feature that, at least in part, bears the imprint of the American model is the provision of a joint (conference) committee of the Senate and the Assembly. That feature—widely practiced though not specifically mentioned in the American Constitution—was acceptable to Debré and others because, in contrast to the American system, it was to be a device used not so much at the behest of the legislature as that of the government.[28]

Finally, there are those who see a similarity between the "French Community"—the collection of former French colonies, mostly in West Africa—and American federalism, in the sense that in areas not clearly specified as coming under the jurisdiction of the French national government (e.g., areas other than foreign policy, defense, and currency) the members of the Community were permitted "residual" autonomy.[29] However, that section of the Constitution could also be seen as imitating the British Commonwealth concept. In any case, this feature soon became a dead letter as virtually all members of the Community opted for independence within two years of the ratification of the Constitution.

For many years, it was argued that no matter how much the national institutional relationships in the Fifth Republic resembled those in the United States, an American type of separation of powers cannot exist in France and hence executive power could not be effectively balanced without a federal system.[30] However, it is possible that a continuation of reforms in the direction of decentralization—reforms that began to be actively promoted in 1981–82, which stop short of federalism—will create patterns of regional-local decision making in France that will lead to a de facto *vertical* balancing of power.

In the 1960s and 1970s, the discussions that were pursued among French political scientists on the theme "Should the Constitution be revised?" frequently referred to the American Constitution.[31] Those who advocated the establishment of a vice president, a non-dissolvable legislature, a limited presidential term, enlarged powers for the Senate, a different type of judicial review, and even federalism, tended to use the American model. Those who wanted to go back to classical parliamentarism used the experience of the United States as an anti-model. Some have argued that, in fact, de Gaulle took a constitution that provided for checks and balances and that in becoming the effective chief of the executive power, he became an American kind of president. In so doing, it has been said, he introduced a "disequilibrium" in his favor because, in contrast to the United States, there is in France no mutual respect between the executive and legislative branches.

The argument about the need to revise the French Constitution began to be revived after the parliamentary elections in March 1986. Until that event, there were no institutions thought capable of setting themselves against the president. The government, from the prime minister to the rest of the cabinet, was a creature of the president, and the Assembly (lower house), controlled by deputies ideologically close to him—many of whom had been elected on the presidential coattails—had no desire to oppose his appointments or policies. However, these elections produced an Assembly controlled by a combination of right-of-center (Gaullist and "Giscardist" liberal or centrist) deputies. This Assembly, and the conservative government that reflects it, had to coexist with a Socialist president, at least until the next presidential elections. The resulting pattern of "cohabitation" is, in effect, an experiment in a checks-and-balances relationship, or a division of power, between president and prime minister that cannot last. Conceivably this situation could culminate in a transformation of the French president from an American-style chief of state to a British-style constitutional monarch.[32] Yet the fact that most French citizens seem to desire that kind of cohabitation suggests that they, like many Americans, have become impatient with the traditional European distinctions between right and left.

Whatever the differences in formal structure between the French and American constitutions, they have not precluded de facto developments of the Fifth Republic in the direction of the American pattern of politics. Such developments have included the combination of the French president's symbolic role with real domestic decision-making responsibilities, a constant growth of the Elysée (presidential palace) staff, the discontinuance of national referenda (and hence a typically Anglo-American avoidance of direct democracy on a national level), the institution of the writ of habeas corpus by legislative means,[33] and an ideological convergence among most political parties, reflecting a widespread American-type consensus about the French political system.

WEST GERMAN CONSTITUTIONALISM AND THE AMERICAN MODEL

The Founding: German Roots and American Influence

In terms of specific textual provisions, the Basic Law of the German Federal Republic is more comparable to the American Constitution than is that of the Fifth Republic. That fact and the circumstances surrounding the writing of the document have led to a widespread conviction that West Germans closely and deliberately followed American constitutional examples. According to Alfred Grosser, "The way the Basic Law came into existence, though it mentioned the Occupation in only the vaguest terms, clearly reflected the primacy of the Occupation powers"[34]—among which, of course, the United States was dominant.

Republican constitutional governments for individual West German provinces (*Länder*) were set up in 1946 at the behest of the American Occupation authorities.[35] Together with their British and French counterparts, the American authorities initiated the convening of a Constituent Assembly (*Parlamentarischer Rat*) in 1948, and members were chosen by the provincial legislatures of the three Western zones of occupation. The Western, and particularly American, influence on the Basic Law could be seen in many ways: the periodic "suggestions" from the military governors in the course of the deliberations; the final letter of approval of the draft constitution in May 1949 (a letter reaffirming that the Occupation statute was superior to the Basic Law); and the initial insistence that the constitution provide for federalism, democratic rule, and a listing of individual rights.

The inclusion of these features has suggested to one scholar that in the Basic Law "one can hear the ring of the language of the United States Constitution."[36] Another scholar has stated, however, that the influence of Americans was "relatively slight" and that "there is nothing in the language of the Basic Law" to warrant the assumption that the American example was followed.[37] It has been argued that West Germans were intent upon propitiating the Americans—not because of specific American directives or because of a desire to kowtow to the major Occupation power, but for other reasons. Some Germans admired the Americans: American democracy somehow seemed beyond flaw and criticism, and the American attitude appeared to be generally supportive. Conversely, it has been asserted that West Germans were so sensitive to public resentment over the Allied military presence—in particular that of Americans—that they tried to avoid giving the impression that they were in any way influenced by the Occupation powers.[38] Which of these arguments is more correct? Certainly, enough precedents existed from Bismarckian Germany for federal patterns, and the Weimar Constitution provided a model of sorts for a bill of rights and for executive responsibility to parliament.

To show that the democratic provisions of the Basic Law have deep German roots, scholars have pointed to the abortive Frankfurt Constitution of 1848–49. Some of the features of that constitution had been inspired by American and French political liberalism. This applied particularly to the bill of rights, many of whose individual provisions (e.g., freedom of speech, assembly, press and religion, and equality before the law) were repeated almost verbatim in the Basic Law.[39]

But perhaps the most important influences on the Bonn Republic's founders were the experiences of the Hitler regime and the "unfortunate" features of the Weimar system. Both of these accounted in large part for the founders' efforts to avoid excessive centralization, to institute guarantees of the republican form of government, and to protect constitutional government against arbitrary use of emergency powers. Most of the participants in the Parliamentary Council were so painfully conscious of the Hitler regime that—without specific American suggestions—they were themselves inclined to opt for federalism, civil liberties, and democracy.

The American influence is apparent, for example, in Article 20, which refers to "separate legislative, executive, and judicial organs." This article, however, probably represented even more a reaction to Nazi theory, according to which all powers—legislative, executive, and judicial—were fused in the person of the Führer.

The negative postwar reaction to Hitler's dictatorship led the drafters of the Basic Law to exaggerate the evil of a strong republican president. They therefore moved further away from the American model by replacing the popularly elected, and relatively powerful, president of the Weimar Republic (1919–33) by a weak chief of state chosen by the national and provincial legislatures.[40] The president's term of office, moreover, was reduced from seven to five years. The presidential feature that appears clearly to have been copied from the United States was the two-term limit of officeholding (Article 54 of the Basic Law). Although the Bonn Republic president is officially a figurehead, with the actual decision-making role in the hands of the prime minister (Chancellor), the president's role has recently been partly "Americanized": the moral leadership position and effectiveness of the presidency have been enhanced under the incumbency of Richard von Weizsäcker—as compared to the political behavior of Chancellor Helmut Kohl, which has been said to verge on moral obtuseness and insensitivity.[41]

An American influence might be partially detected also in the composition of the *Bundesrat*, the upper chamber of parliament: Unlike its predecesssor under the Bismarck Empire (1871–1918), in which the provincial representation had been highly unequal (with Prussia holding more than a third of all seats), the new *Bundesrat* has provided for roughly equal representation—with three to five seats for each province (*Land*). However, the *Bundesrat* differs from the American Senate in that the provinces that it was designed to represent were "not considered a source of state authority on which a constitution be based," as Ludwig Erhard, a member of the Parliamentary Council, put it;[42] hence its legislative power has been much weaker in relation to the *Bundestag* than has been that of the United States Senate in relation to the House of Representatives.

The Constitution as Fundamental Norm

The one matter in which the drafters of the Basic Law were most "mindful of the American example" related to the supremacy of the constitution over statute law.[43] In order to insure that supremacy, the writers of the Basic Law adopted the American idea of judicial review and set up a separate Constitutional Court, which was given the power to nullify acts of parliament. Nevertheless, it has taken quite some time for the Basic Law to establish itself as a *Grundnorm* (fundamental legal standard) in the eyes of Germans.

One German constitutional theorist remarked that the Basic Law departed from the American Constitution in two diametrically opposite ways: On the one hand, the extensive "programmatic," or welfare state, features of the Basic Law that reflected a view of "a planning, guiding, providing, and distributing state"[44]—and that contrasted sharply with the essentially "mechanistic" character of the American Constitution—have been taken very seriously by West German decision makers. On the other hand, many procedural due process and substantive individual rights provisions of the Basic Law have not prevailed easily or quickly over existing prerepublican statute laws. The relative lack of sanctity of the Basic Law, which suggests an underdeveloped "constitutional theology" (*Verfassungstheologie*),[45] can be attributed to a number of factors: (1) a perception of excessive Allied pressures, as well as the fact that the Basic Law was written in the context of incomplete national sovereignty;

(2) the provisional nature of the document, as seen in its being labeled a basic law (*Grundgesetz*) rather than a constitution (*Verfassung*). The premise that the Basic Law was, so to speak, written under duress is implied by the wording of the Preamble, which calls upon "the entire German people to achieve in free self-determination the unity and freedom of Germany." Moreover, as if to underline the absence of a truly popular underpinning of the Basic Law, it was ratified not by referendum but by the provincial legislatures (*Landtage*).[46] Finally (3) there was the attitude of lawyers, judges, and other members of the legal profession, who had been schooled in predemocratic public law (*Staatsrecht*) and showed relatively little comprehension of democratic political norms.

This situation explains why the Basic Law has been amended with far greater frequency—more than three dozen times within thirty years—than the American Constitution.[47] Moreover, the German Constitutional Court was for a long period relatively hesitant to challenge acts of the state or to function as the guardian of individual liberties.

Civil Liberties and Judicial Review

The Basic Law has an impressive bill of rights, but its very provisions have been adulterated by rival provisions limiting these rights to individuals or associations that did not attack "the free democratic order" of the Bonn Republic (Articles 9 [2], 18, 21, [2]). Moreover, the provisions were limited by the continued existence, well into the 1970s, of an Imperial penal code that overprotected the state and gave the police excessive power. Not only did the German Parliament drag its feet in bringing this penal code into conformity with the Basic Law, but it also enacted laws whose effect was to infringe upon the procedural rights, freedom of association, and civil service employment rights of individuals with radical views. The Parliament also passed several constitutional amendments that had the effect of reducing the scope of civil liberties in the interests of stability and security. The West German political and intellectual elite was, at least for the first two decades after the ratification of the Basic Law, less concerned with individual rights than with protecting the authority of the state and of the professional bureaucrats who served it. They continued to view the state and its agents as sacrosanct and awe-inspiring. Thus, while it has been technically easier for citizens in West Germany to appeal to the Constitutional Court—by bringing in a constitutional complaint directly—than for an American citizen to appeal to the Supreme Court, the traditional *Obrigkeitsgefühl* (a public mentality of obeisance to public authorities) and the relative weakness of civil rights organizations have led to an underutilization of the Supreme Court.[48]

The courts on both federal and local levels, reflecting that situation, would often invoke the criminal code (e.g., pertaining to sedition) instead of the Basic Law (protecting free speech) and convict citizens who "defamed" public officials.[49] During the *Spiegel* Affair, which began in the fall of 1962, and in which the publisher of an influential newsmagazine was arrested for having violated an old statutory provision by publishing "seditious" articles, the Constitutional Court refused to rule clearly in favor of the supremacy of freedom of the press (Article 5) over the penal code. Although this action indicated that the majority of the judges had not yet accepted American constitutional tradition, the fact that a dissenting opinion was published (for the first time in the Court's existence) that warned the government against a future abuse of power, suggested that *some* judges had been influenced by the American tradition of judicial assertiveness.[50] Conversely, as the Court was gradually infused with new blood and became more sympathetic to the citizen, there were apparently too many constitutional complaints for the Court to handle. As a result, the rules were changed: it was decided to permit a three-judge panel (out of the eight judges constituting the section, or "senate," dealing with civil liberties—the other section concerning itself with disputes between political levels or institutions) to exercise an American type of certiorari function—and thereby exercise judicial self-restraint—in deciding which petitions had sufficient standing and merit to be submitted.[51] Nevertheless, by the mid–1980s the Constitutional Court had "interpreted about half of the Constitution's 151 articles, and in about 340 cases involving the constitutionality of legislation had invalidated 54 federal and 34 state laws."[52]

It is curious that in one area West Germany's procedural protections for many years went beyond those available in the United States: its statute of limitations on murder. The original Basic Law, like the American Constitution, was silent on the matter of such a statute; it only abolished capital punishment (Article 102) and prohibited prosecution for an act that had not been defined as a crime at the time of commission (Article 103). The enactment of such a statute (or, in point of fact, the retention of the twenty-year limit on prosecution in effect since the enactment of the Imperial German criminal code of 1871) has been, therefore, a purely legislative matter. But for many years the federal government and parliament—while extending the year of expiration of the statute—were reluctant to remove it altogether. Since the authorities were not bothered too much by the existence of other illiberal provisions in the penal code, this reluctance could be attributed not so much to procedural sensitivity as to an unwillingness to try Nazi war criminals. Such an interpretation is given added substance by the fact that the overwhelming majority of those indicted for Nazi crimes have either been acquitted or given ludicrously light sentences.[53] In any case, the abolition of the statute of limitations by act of parliament in 1979 reflected not so much a desire to imitate the United States as the heavy political pressure exerted upon the West German political elite by several Western democratic and East European communist countries.

Significant Divergences from the United States Pattern

Another area in which it is difficult to determine whether the Basic Law goes beyond, or falls short of, the American constitutional arrangement is that of interest groups. There is little doubt that the gradual acceptance in West Germany of the idea that interest-group activity is perfectly legitimate and does not subvert the state, owes much to the American example. Indeed, since the Basic Law explicitly mentions interest groups (unlike the American Constitution, which is silent on this matter) and since laws flowing therefrom provide for the participation of "social partners," the Bonn Republic seems to be more committed to the idea of interest-group politics than the United States. But whereas in America interest-group relationships to public authorities are largely informal—indicating a desire of the groups to retain their private and autonomous character—the Basic Law provision, statutes, and regulations making an official place for interest groups attest to a traditional tendency toward the "officialization" (*Verstaatlichung*) of intermediary bodies. Although that officialization has in practice not diminished the freedom and power of most interest groups, it can be interpreted as a symptom of a statist piety (*Staatsfrômmigkeit*) that is hardly found in the United States.[54]

The asymmetry between West German constitutional features that resemble American ones and "un-American" political traditions and patterns applies also to federalism. On the surface, West German Basic Law parallels the American Constitution with respect to the following: (1) a division of jurisdictions among federal, provincial, and concurrent domains; (2) a bicameral legislature, the upper chamber representing the provinces; and (3) the requirement that the provinces (via the *Bundesrat*) specifically approve constitutional amendments. Yet there remain important differences between West Germany and the United States with respect to the structural manifestations of federalism. Chief among these is the fact that there are no parallel (or separate) civil services and courts to administer and adjudicate only provincial matters. The perpetuation of the traditional unitary administrative and judicial structures reflects the idea that provinces have been not so much autonomous as "privileged provinces" or administrative units (*Verwaltungsstaaten*).[55]

Whatever American constitutional influence there may have been on West German federalism, judicial review, and civil liberties, it has not obscured the more traditional German and continental European features that still exist, such as the parliamentary system with its fusion of power, the dual executive, the Roman law system, and the role of established churches. Secondly, there is the specific mention of political parties, a feature that (whether or not it reflects the important practical role of parties in the American system) parallels the clear textual reference to that institution in the postwar constitutions of France, Italy, and (to a lesser extent) Austria. Thirdly, whereas the Bill of Rights was not included in the United States Constitution by America's founding fathers, the list of civil liberties takes up the first twenty articles of the Basic Law. The last of them (Article 20) even affirms the right to resist attempts [by governments] to establish an unconstitutional order. Fourthly, the Basic Law goes far beyond anything contained in the American Constitution in the self-imposed circumscription of national freedom of action: in Article 24, which allows the federal government to transfer sovereignty to international organizations and regional groupings; in Article 25, which subjects it to the rules of international law; and in Article 26, which defines the preparation for an aggressive war as an unconstitutional act. Finally, there are the constitutional legislative emergency clauses (Articles 67, 68, and 81) which serve as a witness to the fact that the Basic Law—unlike the American Constitution—was written with memories of the recent history of brutal dictatorship in mind, within the context of the Cold War, and under the specter of a continued division of Germany.

To what degree will America's constitutional influence be felt in the future in West Germany? On the one hand, the operation of the West German constitutional system is likely to be modified in an American direction because of the impact of a more democratized social system and the increasing modernization of the political culture. On the other hand, the fact that the Basic Law, with all its democratic provisions, came into being under Allied occupation and was put into effect within the context of American dominance, the North Atlantic connection, and West German prosperity, raises an interesting question. Could constitutional democracy in West Germany survive any of the following situations: a weakening of America's global influence, a sudden steep rise in unemployment or other serious economic dislocations, and a German departure from NATO? The answer to this question will tell us much about the extent American constitutional values have been internalized by West German society.

SUMMARY

Both the Constitution of the French Fifth Republic and the Basic Law of the German Federal Republic contain features that are common to Western democratic systems: a delineation of functions of executive, legislative, and judicial branches; a means of popular participation in the selection of governing personnel; mechanisms for the peaceful transfer of power and the resolution of inter-institutional conflicts; a limitation of governmental prerogatives and, as a corollary, a bill of rights—either clearly specified and detailed (as in West Germany) or implied and brief (as in the Fifth Republic). We can speak of these features as "American" in the sense that the American Constitution has embodied them for longer, and in a more continuous fashion, than have French or German constitutions.

The current constitutions of France and West Germany, as this discussion has shown, do not parallel the American document in all particulars. Nor was this possible, given the unique political histories of the two countries and their indigenous constitutional traditions. The American Constitution was written in the eighteenth century, an age of "classical" liberalism, when the ideal was a government susceptible to control and interested in intervening only minimally in the affairs of citizens. The Fifth Republic and West German constitutions, in contrast, are products of the twentieth century, when governments are widely viewed as instruments for responding, directly and democratically, to the economic and social needs of the people. Nevertheless, French and West German constitutional interpreters continue, with increasing frequency, to refer to the American Constitution as a yardstick and, in doing so, often adapt American political values to their own conditions.

NOTES

The author wishes to thank Lawrence W. Beer and Richard B. Wilson for their comments and suggestions from which he profited immensely.

1. For a general discussion of the distinctions between mechanistic and programmatic constitutions, see Karl Loewenstein, *Political Power and the Governmental Process*, 2nd. ed. (Chicago: University of Chicago Press, 1963), 136–43.

2. See Leslie Derfler, *President and Parliament: A Short History of the French Presidency* (Boca Raton, Fla.: University Presses of Florida, 1983), 86–87.

3. Ibid.

4. See Hughes Tay, *Le régime présidentiel et la France* (Paris: Librairie Générale de Droit et de Jurisprudence, 1967), 95–96.

5. Carl J. Friedrich, "The New French Constitution: Political and Historical Perspectives," *Harvard Law Review* 72, no. 5 (March 1959): 806.

6. See *Travaux préparatoires de la constitution: Avis et débats du comité consultatif constitutionnel* (Paris: Documentation Française, 1960). This is not a verbatim report but an analytical summary containing occasional simplifications and distortions.

7. Michel Debré, "The Constitution of 1958: Its Raison d'Être and How it Evolved," in William G. Andrew and Stanley Hoffman, eds., *The Fifth Republic At Twenty* (Albany: State University of New York Press, 1981), 17.

8. Derfler, *President and Parliament*, 129.

9. Michel Debré, *La république et son pouvoir* (Paris, 1950), 89–96; and Michel Debré and Emmanuel Monick, *Refaire la France* (Paris: Plon, 1945), 120.

10. This point was made by Friedrich, "The New French Constitution," 811–12.

11. It might even be argued that the French Constitution's wording is more republican than that of the United States Constitution, since the latter (in Article 4, Sec. 4) provides merely that "the United States shall guarantee to every state in this union a republican form of government," and that the term "republican form" has had no identifiable meaning in United States law but is a purely political definition (Cf. *Luther v. Borden*, 1849).

12. Cited in Maurice C. J. Vile, *Constitutionalism and the Separation of Powers* (Oxford: Clarendon Press, 1967), 257.

13. Ibid., 85.

14. See ibid., 6.

15. Vile, *Constitutionalism and the Separation of Powers*, 209.

16. Max Beloff, "The Separation of Powers in the Constitution of the Fifth Republic," *Parliamentary Affairs* 12, no. 1 (1958–59): 37–46.

17. Vile, *Constitutionalism and the Separation of Powers*, 61.

18. See "Max Weber on Law" in *Economy and Society* (Cambridge, Mass.: Harvard University Press, 1954), 335; and discussion in *Max Weber: An Intellectual Portrait*, ed. Reinhard Bendix (Garden City, N.Y.: Doubleday Anchor, 1962), chap. XIII ("Legal Domination: The Modern State and the Struggle for Power"), esp. 440–441.

19. *United States v. Curtiss-Wright Export Corp.* 229 U.S. 304 (1936).

20. Nicholas Wahl, "Aux origines de la nouvelle constitution," *Revue française de science politique* 9, no. 1 (1959): 39–40.

21. See Mauro Cappelletti and William Cohen, *Comparative Constitutional Law: Cases and Materials* (Indianapolis and New York: Bobbs-Merrill, 1979), 45–46.

22. Ibid.

23. 1 Cranch 137 (1803).

24. On this point, see Kenneth C. Wheare, *Modern Constitutions*, 2nd. ed. (London: Oxford University Press, 1966), 125–26.

25. See Valéry Giscard d'Estaing, *2 Francais sur 3* (Paris- Flammarion, 1984).

26. It is instructive here to refer by way of comparison to the unimpeded long tenure of Hindenburg as president (1925–34) and the even longer tenures of Bismarck (1862–90) and Adenauer (1949–63) as chancellors in Germany.

27. Michel Debré, Georges Pompidou, Jacques Chaban-Delmas, Jacques Chirac, and Raymond Barre.

28. *Travaux préparatoires*, 174–78, 190–91. The Consultative Committee had originally wanted either chamber to be able to call for a joint committee.

29. Friedrich, "The New French Constitution," 832.

30. Ibid., 815; and Derfler, *President and Parliament*, 175.

31. See, for example, *Revue politique et parlementaire*, 66e année, nos. 741–44 (January, February, March, April 1964).

32. See Patrick Auvret, "La faculté d'empêcher un président de la République, *Revue du droit public et de la science politique*, no. 1 (1986): 141–168.

33. A government bill providing for habeas corpus protections, supported by

all four major political parties, was passed in 1984 and became effective as of January 1, 1985.

34. Alfred Grosser, *The Federal Republic of Germany* (New York: Praeger, 1964), 16.

35. For example, in the Länder Bavaria, Hesse, and Württemberg-Baden. See *Verfassung des Landes Hessen und Grundgesetz für die Bundesrepublik Deutschland*, no author (Bad Homburg: Verlag Dr. Max Gehlen, 1957), 16–23.

36. Peter H. Merkl, *The Origin of the West German Republic* (New York: Oxford University Press, 1963), 10. Cf. Grosser, *The Federal Republic of Germany*, 16.

37. John F. Golay, *The Founding of the Federal Republic of Germany* (Chicago: University of Chicago Press, 1958), 108, 176. See also Carl J. Friedrich, "The Political Theory of the New Democratic Constitutions," in Arnold J. Zurcher, ed., *Constitutions and Constitutional Trends Since World War II* (New York: New York University Press, 1951), 20.

38. Peter Merkl, *Germany: Yesterday and Tomorrow* (New York: Oxford University Press, 1965), 150. See also Carl J. Friedrich, *The Impact of American Constitutionalism Abroad* (Boston: Boston University Press, 1967), 68.

39. See *Demokratie als Auftrag: Drei Jahrzehnte Bundesrepublik Deutschland* (Bonn: Presse- und Informationsamt der Bundesregierung, 1979), 20–25. See also Thomas Ellwein, *Das Regierungssystem der Bundesrepublik Deutschland* (Cologne: Westdeutscher Verlag, 1963), who argues (53–54) that the "federalist" features of the 1848 constitution that leaned on the American Constitution had been based on a misunderstanding of that document.

40. Actually, the electoral agency is the Federal Assembly (*Bundesversammlung*), composed of all members of the *Bundestag* (lower house) plus an equal number of individuals chosen by the provincial legislatures, for a total of nearly 1,000 electors.

41. Following the "Bitburg Affair" (President Reagan's visit in May 1985 to a West German military cemetery containing the graves of S.S. officers), some German commentators argued that the constitutional division of roles between the chancellor and the president was being obscured and partially reversed in practice. Cf. Gunter Hofmann, "Der Präses und der Populist," and Hans Schuler, "Die Verlockung, über den Zaun zu fressen," in *Die Zeit*, May 31, 1985, p. 3.

42. U.S. Office of Military Government, *Documents on the Creation of the German Federal Constitution* (Berlin, 1949), 79.

43. Grosser, *The Federal Republic of Germany*, 21.

44. Eberhard Menzel, "Die Sozialstaatlichkeit als Verfassungsprinzip der Bundesrepublik," in *Der bügerliche Rechtsstaat*, ed. Mehdi Tohidipur (Frankfurt: Suhrkamp, 1978), 321.

45. Menzel, "Die Sozialstaatlichkeit," 342–43. See also Jürgen Seifert, *Grundgesetz und Restauration* (Darmstadt: Luchterhand, 1974), 7–8, 11.

46. On the lack of popular enthusiasm for the Basic Law, see Karl-Heinz Jansen, "Das dauerhafte Provisorium," *Die Zeit*, May 24, 1974, p. 10.

47. One source (*Demokratie als Auftrag*, 110) specified 34 amendments between 1949 and 1979; according to another source (Seifert, *Grundgesetz*, 7–8), during the period 1949–74, 45 articles were amended (some more than once), 35 were newly added, and 5 were abolished, and altogether 350 changes were made in the text.

48. American *policy* (as distinct from American constitutional example) contributed to that situation. In October 1945, the four occupying powers had issued a directive that the German judicial system to be reestablished, base itself on democracy and on the principles of due process and not guilt by analogy or the "sound instinct of the people." Directives issued later called for the establishment of a civil service that would be open to all segments of the population and behave in a nonpartisan fashion. Ironically, American occupation officials themselves contributed to the imperfect "Americanization" of administrative and judicial patterns by commuting the sentences of many Nazi bureaucrats and judges and facilitating their reentry into the civil service and the courts. See Karl Loewenstein, "Justice," in Edward H. Litchfield, ed., *Governing Postwar Germany* (Ithaca, N.Y.: Cornell University Press, 1953), 245–55.

49. One of these laws, which remained on the books until the 1970s, had been promulgated during the Hitler regime.

50. See Donald R. Kommers, "The Spiegel Affair," in Theodore L. Becker, ed., *Political Trials* (Indianapolis and New York: Bobbs-Merrill, 1971), 5–33.

51. Cappelletti and Cohen, *Comparative Constitutional Law*, 441. On judicial self-restraint, see also Klaus von Beyme, "The Power Structure in the Federal Republic," in *Contemporary Germany: Politics and Culture*, ed. Charles Burdick et al. (Boulder, Colo.: Westview Press, 1985), 88.

52. David P. Conradt, *The German Polity*, 3rd ed. (New York and London: Longman, 1986), 205.

53. See R. M. W. Kempner, *Ein Wag aus der Vergangenheit* (Frankfurt: Ullstein, 1969). In 1969, the Parliament voted to extend the statute of limitations to 30 years from the beginning of the Bonn Republic, that is, to 1979.

54. Hans-Jürgen Puhle, "Innovation von oben," in überforderte Demokratie? *Grundfragen des demokratischen Prozesses*, no editor, Offene Welt Nr. 103/1975 (Frankfurt: Wirtschaftspolitische Gesellschaft von 1947, 1975), 26–28.

55. Ellwein, *Das Regierungssystem*, 54.

5

The Influence of American Constitutionalism in Asia

Lawrence W. Beer

Lawrence W. Beer finds widespread influence of American constitutionalism in certain Asian countries framing constitutions since the close of World War II. Japan more than any other Asian nation was affected by American constitutionalism because, as in the case of Germany, the United States was an occupying power at the time the postwar constitution was written in 1947. Besides Japan, the Philippines, South Korea, and India were strongly influenced by American constitutionalism but for different reasons. Beer compares in broad terms the American and Asian constitutional traditions and points out reasons for certain similarities and differences.

Each country has a distinctive constitutional history and culture, but only a few have enriched the world's constitutional culture with basic ideas, institutions, approaches to law, and national experiences. The United States is one such contributor to constitutionalism. The Declaration of Independence, the Constitution of the United States, a few other documents, and seminal judicial decisions bounding the directions of constitutional development are peculiar to their times and place, but they have also affected modern statecraft and legalism, especially since the demise of colonialism after World War II.[1] Many Asian countries have taken the American experience into account when developing their own constitutionalism, and Japan, the Philippines, and India have been profoundly influenced.

United States constitutionalism remains an important reference point because of America's power, but also because many Asians accept the inherent transcultural value of a few elements in America's approach to democratic government and law. Such elements include the following: a single-document national constitution, usually with a preamble of guiding principles, as a means of fusing ideas with law and governmental institutions; a listing of constitutional rights defended by independent courts; the idea of a constitution as "the supreme law of the land"; a constituent or constitutional assembly with authority to develop a basic law which legitimizes independent statehood, a revolution, or some other form of major sociopolitical change; and the concept of the separation of powers.

T. K. K. Iyer of Singapore suggests that even where American influence is not obvious, Western domination of the world press assures attention to American ideas:

> It is in the realm of constitutional ideals that the American experience captures the Asian imagination (and indeed the rest of the world). This is so even where Asians are critical of developments in American Constitutional Law and Practice. ... [M]ost of us are apt to overlook the historic antiquity of the foundation documents of the Constitution of USA because we have the image of USA as a "new" country that came into prominence after World War II.... [W]hat accounts for the contemporary influence of American ideals is the extensive coverage American constitutional and legal discussions receive in the world press and media. I do think this is a decisive factor. Many people in Asia know more about U.S. Constitutional matters than they do about, perhaps [those of] any other foreign nation.[2]

The sixty percent of humankind living in the span between Japan and Pakistan directly absorbed Western ideas of law and constitutionalism more from British and continental European sources than from the United States until the recent decades of worldwide constitutional experimentation.[3] Europe controlled most of Asia in colonial times. The exceptions were: the Philippines, under American control from around 1900; Japan, free of unequal Western treaties from about 1900; Taiwan and Korea, Japan's modern possessions until after World War II; and Thailand, sandwiched between British Burma and French "Indochina." The French dominated what is now Vietnam, Kampuchea, and Laos; the Netherlands controlled the islands of the "Dutch East Indies," now Indonesia; the British empire included South Asian territories and today's Malaysia and Singapore; and these and other European imperialist countries joined in the exploitation of China.[4]

For some perspective on the constitutions of the United States, Asia, and the world, consider that of 164 single-document constitutions in effect as of January 1986, only twenty-two dated earlier than 1950.[5] Very few countries, such as Norway (1814) and Colombia (1886), continue with constitutions of the nineteenth century, and only the United States Constitution has been in force since the eighteenth century. What is even more thought-provoking is that over one hundred of today's constitutions trace their origins only as far back as 1970. In every continent, constitutional experimentation and change continue in pursuit of stable order.

In Asia's constitutional chronology, only four nations have basic laws written as early as the 1940s: Japan, whose 1947 Constitution has yet to be amended; the Republic of China, 1947, written for China but in force only on Taiwan, along with martial law of varying degree since 1949; Indonesia, 1945, but with two other constitutions in effect between 1949 and 1959; and India, whose Constitution of 1950 has been amended over forty times.[6] Other current constitutions were adopted as follows: Afghanistan, 1980; Bangladesh, 1972; Bhutan, 1953; Brunei, 1984; Burma, 1974; China, 1982;. Kampuchea (Cambodia), 1981; Laos, 1975; Malaysia, 1963; Mongolia, 1960; Nepal, 1962; North Korea, 1972; Pakistan, 1973; Papua–New Guinea, 1975; the Philippines, 1986; Singapore, 1963; South Korea, 1980; Sri Lanka, 1978; Thailand, 1978; and Vietnam, 1980.

SOME MEANINGS OF "CONSTITUTIONALISM"

Apart from the few Asian communist states, countries of the region commonly subscribe to a mixture of democratic socialism with indigenous religious and ethical systems, but in a kaleidoscopic variety of ways. The terms "democracy" and "constitutionalism" as discussed in the United States appear to represent a culture-bound, sometimes unclear, definition and do not always provide sufficient distinctions about constitutionalism for purposes of analyzing contemporary Asian state systems. To preface comments on American constitutional influence in Asia, an explanation of some usage and working definitions is in order. Distinctions must be made between "documentary constitutionalism," "democracy," "constitutionalism," "constitutional democracy," and "nonconstitutionalism."[7]

Every Asian country has chosen to adopt documentary constitutionalism—that is, to use as its most basic formal law a single national document setting forth the major divisions, structures, principles, and powers of its government, and the rights and duties of its citizens. Even if the language of the constitution is a reasonably plain guide to the intentions and practices of a government and a people, detailed knowledge of the country's history and social culture may be needed for an accurate and fair understanding of a specific constitutional issue. In other cases, the relationship between constitutional provisions and practices may be obscured or so tenuous as to elude the educated observer. Nevertheless, it is not a trivial United States contribution that such statements of basic law have become for the first time a shared institution of world legal culture, as nations pursue stability, development, and constitutional arrangements that best express their identities and meet their needs.

The use of the term "democracy" here is restricted to governments grounded in popular sovereignty and in majority decision-making processes. Democracy is not the antithesis of authoritarianism insensitive to individual rights—it makes the expressed will of the majority the determinative political value—nor is it simply recognition of inherent individual dignity or some other restraining public value. Excluded from this definition are state systems in which the majority merely acquiesces or accepts a government and/or its actions without a legitimizing process of direct voting or an election of leaders who vote. Communist states and other nations in which political participation and voting do not involve free majority decision making and personal choice also fall outside the definition of democracy.

"Constitutionalism" as here defined connotes a division and limitation of power under law more unequivocally than democracy, but not necessarily an overriding commitment to individual rights or some other single public value. Constitutionalism is taken to mean principled restraint under law of the power, even the democratic power, of all in government. Powers are defined and limited in a generally recognized, predictable manner by written and/or unwritten basic rules. In a "constitutional democracy," the government is democratic but also recognizes as most fundamental the value of each person. The state's preoccupation is with service of the individual person in the community and with the protection and promotion of human rights, and not with the pleasure of the majority. Other constitutionalist systems are grounded in different values and principles which legitimize and limit power. In Asia, the appeal and influence of American constitutionalism lies not in American democracy per se, but in America insofar as it is a constitutional democracy committed to a full panoply of individual rights based on the supreme public value of the individual. The tension in American constitutional dialogue seems to have been between democracy and constitutional democracy, and over which human rights should be made into legal rights. Asian constitutionalists, on the other hand, have tried to deal with the tensions between indigenous constitutional foundations and constitutional democracy in the light of national needs.

Among the alternative foundation values which have limited somewhat the traditional scope and legitimate exercise of power and have affected modern Asian constitutionalist thought have been the following: state harmony and justice by adherence to Confucian social ethics under a monarch who is assumed to possess a mandate to rule from Heaven based on his virtue (e.g., the kings of traditional China, Korea, and Vietnam; and the current leaders of those countries and Sinic Singapore);[8] service in accord with the Will of Allah (e.g., heavily Islamic states such as Pakistan, Bangladesh, Malaysia, and Indonesia);[9] peace, order, and prosperity in the state and society by kingly observance of legitimizing rituals and attention to the implications for statecraft of certain numbers, dates, and directions on the compass (e.g., the Brahmanic and Buddhist monarchies of South and Southeast Asia);[10] and service of a national community conceived of as a uniquely sacred collectivity (e.g., prewar Japan).[11]

Here the terms "constitutionalism" and "nonconstitutionalism" are used to refer to both theory and practice. A nonconstitutionalist state is one where the power of the government is not clearly limited, but absolute or extremely vague in scope and unpredictable in its exercise. Analysis of the status of constitutionalism in a country requires attention not only to its constitutional ideals but to its progress toward or away from their achievement. One must also understand both of the above in terms of influential traditional theories or practices and specify which aspect of constitutionalism is the focus of interest. Whether or not in earlier or more recent history the laws, institutions, and generally accepted political values of a country have been constitutionalist is an empirical question. Relatively few detailed interdisciplinary studies exist of constitutionalism in Asian nations to permit any fair and precise judgments. Of course, judgments are relatively easier where a country's failure to measure up to its own constitutionalist standards are large-scale, continuing, and systematic, but many constitutional systems in Asia defy any such simple assessment. As in the United States, the relationships between formal law and the Constitution, theories and popular myths, ideals and practice, are sometimes bafflingly complex. Nevertheless, constitutional democracy—the ideal in terms of which American constitutionalism has generally seemed most relevant in Asia—can be summarized in terms of such practical measures as:

1. A division of governmental power among two or more organs;
2. Some form of independent judicial system with jurisdiction over cases involving civil rights and liberties;
3. Regularized limits on the amount of governmental power possessed by anyone and upon the length of time power may be legitimately held; democratic elections, with a secret ballot, to assure peaceful, routine passage from one national leader or group of leaders to the next and to guarantee public agreement on the legitimacy and composition of the leadership;

4. Governmental authority and means of coercion under law sufficient to maintain public peace and national security within limits defined by the human rights of citizens;
5. Governmental involvement in socioeconomic problem solving in order to meet citizen needs for food, clothing, shelter, security, and a life compatible with human dignity, insofar as the private sector fails to meet these needs;
6. Legally protected and encouraged freedom of peaceful expression and a right to silence; tolerance regarding personal or group belief or opinion;
7. Procedural rights in criminal justice and civil law for each citizen equal to those of all others in the national community;
8. Establishment by the government and acceptance by the public at large of the country's constitution as the supreme law of the land.

THE NATURE AND LIMITS OF AMERICAN INFLUENCE ON CONSTITUTIONALISM IN ASIA

The colonial centuries left all the subregions of Asia (with the exception of the Philippines) with understandings of modern law and institutions of government heavily influenced by British, French, Dutch, Spanish, German, and preexisting practices. Before 1945, American constitutionalism was not irrelevant but only of occasional or minor importance in Asia. Granting the primacy of other sources, American constitutional ideas were of interest to modern Asian nationalists dreaming of independence and new kinds of statehood. To them, as to the Europeans from whom they learned, the American experience was an integral part of the Western political heritage.

A comparison of some features of constitutionalism in Asia and the United States will provide a context for the discussion of American influence which follows. In Asia, *freedom* has been valued by many governments and peoples, but *equality* has been emphasized even more strongly. This is so based on general principles and because many citizens have suffered severely from poverty, maldistribution of wealth, lack of opportunity, and economic exploitation.[12] Economic justice and national development have been accorded higher priority than property rights among Asian friends of constitutional democracy. Asian elites, in and out of government, generally have seen no necessary linkage between a free enterprise system and individual rights and freedoms, in contradistinction to many Americans. Many Asians inclined toward anticommunist democratic constitutionalism have separated economic liberty from political and social freedoms, and have felt the latter deserve more vigilant protection. In many Asian countries, there was a consensus, a pragmatic democratic socialism.

Freedom of the press and other forms of freedom of expression have been more frequently restricted in some parts of Asia than in the United States on grounds that they threaten public peace, security, and national development. Some of these justifications have not simply been nonconstitutionalist authoritarianism, though others have been. In fairness, Americans should be cautious in passing judgment on such matters, but torture or prolonged incarceration without trial for peaceable political dissent is always incompatible with democratic constitutionalism.

The Islamic countries and the Philippines, like the United States, emphasize monotheism, while Hinduism, Buddhism, Taoism, animism, and other belief systems have different religious roots. A multitude of ethnic or religious divisions have made tolerance an even higher priority of constitutionalism in many South and Southeast Asian nations than in America. Consider, for example, the communal tensions between the Chinese and Malays in Malaysia; between the Sikhs, Muslims, and Hindus of India; and between the Sinhalese and Tamils in Sri Lanka. The American principle of protecting religious liberty and somehow maintaining distance between the state and religion was broadly understood in Asia. Yet many Asians, like many Europeans, have found some American interpretations of separation of church and state strained, convoluted, inconsistent, and at times even hostile to religion itself in favor of a somewhat rigid secularism.[13] The more common concern in Asia was not whether a particular religion was established—for the wisdom of establishment depends on local factors—but whether constitutional law and the state could protect tolerance against discrimination and allow friendly respectful treatment to all religions.

The military has had a greater impact on constitutionalism in some Asian nations than in the United States for many reasons: international war left such men in a privileged position they were loath to relinquish; they sometimes refused to abide by constitutional government; they had once filled a vacuum as the government's main source of professionalized administrators and had grown accustomed to positions of power; they controlled the ruling party and the means of coercion; or, in some instances, they wanted to clean up corruption or disorder.[14] The mix of reasons has varied from country to country, but at one time or another, generals or retired generals have ruled from Pakistan, Bangladesh, Burma, and Indonesia to Thailand and South Korea, and have deeply affected politics in other nations, such as Taiwan, the Philippines, and China. Martial law has put constitutionalism in abeyance or at best in an ambiguous position. Taiwan, for example, was under such military rule longer than any other nation, from 1949 until recently; but even on Taiwan the rigor of controls varied over time. Some tendency toward democratic constitutionalism developed in an uneasy parallel there with martial law, and in October 1986, the ruling Nationalist Party finally announced an end to martial law.[15] Japan's explicit constitutional exclusion of the military from government, in reaction to the 1945 defeat and to repressive prewar militarism, has contributed to the maintenance of constitutional democracy.[16] Whether Asian armed services will in the future serve or inhibit constitutionalism is not clear. To date, however, the importance of the military in many countries has been more as government administrators than as armed forces leaders, and in this respect they stand in sharp contrast to the American military.

The legislative systems of Asia have also owed much more to the British or continental European parliamentary tradition than to the American model. Prime ministers and their cabinets were the common form of executive in such lands as India, Japan, Malaysia, Singapore, and Thailand. A strong presidency characterized other systems such as Pakistan, Sri Lanka, Indonesia, the Philippines, Taiwan, and South Korea. In communist countries a few party leaders ruled, and subordinate governmental agencies administered the system. Only the presidencies of Indonesia and the Philippines were originally modeled in part on that of the United States.[17] A rich tradition of monarchies, some of them constitutionalist monarchies, continues in Japan, Malaysia, Nepal, the Himalayan principalities, Brunei, Thailand, and, though now under Vietnamese dominance, Laos and Kampuchea. In Malaysia, for example, the king is elected for a five-year term from among the nine hereditary sultans on the thirteen-member Conference of Rulers.[18]

In Asia, only Malaysia and India share a form of federalism with the United States, although Indonesia experimented with "the United States of Indonesia" in 1950.[19] The eminent jurist Tun Mohamed Suffian has compared the American and Malaysian experiments:

> [I]n the United States the Constitution spells out what powers "are delegated" to the centre "nor prohibited" to states and provides that anything not so delegated to the centre nor prohibited to the states is reserved to the states respectively or to the people. The Malaysian Constitution... follows the Indian Constitution in providing for a federal list, a state list, and a concurrent list, which spell out in great detail federal subjects, state subjects, and concurrent subjects with respect to which the federation, the states, and both... respectively, have legislative and executive power, and further in providing in Article 77 that residual power on subjects not in the lists shall be vested in states. (Malaysia is a small country, and needs a strong central government; thus subjects like the police and education... are federal....)[20]

India's federal structure was built with an eye on several precedents: its own experience under the British Government of India Act (1935), the Australian and Canadian federal systems, and that of the United

States.[21] Distinctive features include the power of the central government to dissolve a state government and rule directly, and the ability of Parliament to legislate on any matter on the state list of subjects under Article 249, if the upper house has first passed by a two-thirds majority a resolution declaring it "necessary or expedient in the national interest."[22] This latter provision was inspired by B. N. Rau's discussions on constitutional problems with Americans during a visit to the United States.[23]

Probably the most appreciated American institution as a contribution to constitutional culture in some Asian countries has been that of an independent judicial system with the power to determine the constitutionality of acts of government. Judicial review has become a credible mechanism for enforcing constitutional rights and rules in a number of Asian legal systems and a respected possibility in others. Influenced by the United States, judicial review was written into the constitutions of Japan and India and has had an enormous impact on national life. In Japan and elsewhere, the coexistence of judicial review with a civil law tradition has at times limited the constitutional jurisdiction of the judges but not their independence as judges. German, Swiss, and French legal thinking and approaches to judicial decision making have also influenced Japan, Taiwan, Thailand, and South Korea, and Dutch law has affected Indonesia and Sri Lanka. Thus, foreign influences on Asian law (other than those of the United States) have been many.

As a general rule, supreme courts are not coequal branches of government in Asia. Moreover, both English common law parliamentarism and civil law deference to democratic parliaments have added to political factors restraining judicial application of constitutional provisions to cases in controversy. In contrast, P. K. Tripathi of India has maintained that excessive reliance on the courts to settle issues better left to legislatures has had a negative effect at times on the development of statutes for rights protection in his country.[24] Such problems notwithstanding, in India, and through India in Malaysia, Sri Lanka, and other countries, judicial review has been a boon to limited, responsible government and human rights. The Philippine Supreme Court—especially before the 1972 imposition of martial law and since the 1986 "People's Revolution"—was also able to exercise judicial review on behalf of democratic constitutionalism.

The ways of changing constitutions vary strikingly in Asia. Like the United States, Indonesia has had a short constitution and has been reluctant to amend it. Japan has yet to pass an amendment under its rigorous processes, but this situation troubles only a relatively small minority. On the other hand, India's Constitution is book-length and has been amended forty-two times—by a simple majority with "a majority of not less than two-thirds of the members" of each house "present and voting."[25] Although modeled on India's process, Malaysia's amendment procedures have different requirements for different categories of amendment, and seventeen amendments had been passed at the time of this writing. More important in Asia have been the replacements of entire constitutions in the past fifteen years, as noted earlier.[26]

Bearing in mind this background on Asian constitutionalism and government systems, where, when, and how does American constitutional influence fit into the constitutional development of Asia? In Japan, Korea, and the Philippines, American occupation yielded quite different results. More common as a context for American influence has been Asian consultation of seminal American constitutional documents, scholarly writings about United States constitutionalism and law, judicial decisions, and meetings with individual American scholars. This consultation took place at the origins of the constitutions of some countries and continued thereafter in others. Consultations with American experts have occurred in Asia and in the United States, with Asians sometimes traveling to the United States and in other cases Americans visiting Asia.

It is not simply the Constitution of the United States alone, or in combination with other basic documents, that has represented American democratic constitutionalism which some Asians have found important enough to study and use in their own countries. It is rather the perceived powerful commitment to limited and responsive government, to human rights and dignity, and to the independence and equality of all the earth's peoples which has inspired Asians. Admittedly, the degree of that commitment within the United States may not have equaled the commitment in the same cause of many of the Asians who looked to the American experience for guidance. But the commitment, however imperfect, was embodied in those American documents, institutions, laws, and judicial holdings which have been on the side of democratic constitutionalism.

A few examples will indicate the parameters of American influence. In Asia as elsewhere, a country's constitutionalism cannot be understood solely or even primarily in terms of the words of a constitution, but only by consulting the most authoritative contemporary interpretations of its law and constitution in light of a nation's fundamental value commitments.

Southeast Asia

Although they do not set forth the details of governmental structure and citizen rights, two documents have probably inspired many more in Asia and the United States than the American Constitution itself—the Declaration of Independence and Abraham Lincoln's Gettysburg Address. In Southeast Asia, for example, the Indonesian Nationalist Party

(PNI) in 1927 was proclaimed on July 4 in conscious commemoration of the Declaration. In the decades before Indonesian independence, speeches and political posters quoted phrases from the Declaration and the Gettysburg Address as words appropriate for people everywhere supporting the cause of anticolonialist democracy.[27]

It is sometimes hard to properly place one piece in the puzzle among the many influences in drafting a constitution. Framers of the Constitution of Indonesia, however, were known to have consulted the American experience. One of them, Mohammed Yamin, conveyed the respect with which American documents and principles were regarded:

> Before me is the structure of the Republic of the United States of America, which time and again has been used as an example for several constitutions in the world, for this is the oldest constitution existing in the world and contains three elements: (1) the Declaration of Rights in the city of Philadelphia (1774); (2) the Declaration of Independence of July 4, 1776; (3) finally, the Constitution of the United States of America (1787).[28]

The Preamble of the "Constitution of the Proclamation State," as it is called by Indonesians, is reminiscent of the Declaration of Independence in referring to both God and independence from the former mother country:

> Whereas Independence is the natural right of every nation, colonialism must be abolished in this world because it is not in conformity with Humanity and Justice.
>
> And the struggle of the movement for the Independence of Indonesia has now reached the hour of rejoicing by leading the People of Indonesia safe and sound to the gateway of the Independence of an Indonesian State which is free, united, sovereign, just and prosperous.
>
> Thanks to the blessing of God Almighty and impelled by the noble desire to lead their own free national life, the People of Indonesia hereby declare their independence.[29]

The text continues with the *Pancasila*, the Five Principles or pillars of Indonesian ideology: belief in one God; a just and civilized humanism; the unity of Indonesia, with its 165 million people, hundreds of subcultures, and over 13,500 islands; democracy based on consultation and representation; and social justice for all. In practice, President Suharto and his Golkar coalition have ruled with little governmental change since 1966.

With respect to the Philippines, the United States reimposed control just as the colonies were gaining freedom from Spain. As in the Occupation of Japan after World War II, America used its time of control to institutionalize American understandings of law and constitution. The United States also promoted public health and education but left the wealth of the country in the hands of an exploitive few. Independence came on July 4, 1946, as had been promised in 1934. The constitution approved by Americans and the Filipinos in 1935 became the "supreme law" of the land from 1946 until martial law was declared in 1972.[30] From 1972 until 1986, the government of President Ferdinand Marcos added irregular authoritarianism to problems of economic injustice and political instability. Martial law was lifted and new constitutional features introduced in 1981 and 1984, but authoritarianism and pervasive corruption continued.[31] The "People's Revolution" of President Corazon Aquino in the elections of 1986 led to reinstitution of constitutional democracy and to the exile of Marcos. On October 12, 1986, a broadly representative Constitutional Commission approved a draft constitution for submission to a plebiscite in early 1987. The new Constitution of the Philippines would restore and go beyond democratic traditions influenced by America that were in place before the Marcos era. The president, for example, would remain strong but would serve only one six-year term and could not appoint relatives to public office; extensive rights provisions were expanded to include workers' right to unionize, and to ban capital punishment; the Supreme Court's authority to declare laws and official acts unconstitutional was extended to matters previously reserved for the executive ("political questions"); legislative power was restored to a bicameral Congress. In July 1987 the new constitution came into force.[32]

South Asia

The United States depository of constitutional wisdom has also been consciously rejected by some constitutionalists in Asia. When Sir Ivor Jennings was drafting Sri Lanka's "Soulbury Constitution" in the 1940s, for example, he somewhat arrogantly opposed an American-style Bill of Rights as superfluous, because Britain had "no Bill of Rights: we merely have liberty according to law, and we think—truly, I believe—that we do the job better than any country."[33] After independence, the lack of constitutional rights provisions made Sri Lankan judges rely on law and judicial precedent to affirm individual rights. They drew some precedents from India and the United States.[34] The later Constitutions of 1972 and 1978, however, have contained declarations of rights which have "provided a radical break from the British tradition. . . . [They are] reminiscent of the Constitutions of the United States, Ireland and India and of certain countries in Europe."[35]

South Asian constitutionalists have also solicited the views of American legal scholars and judges. One example was the series of discussions Albert P. Blaustein and other Americans had with leaders of Bangladesh, such as Kamal Hossein and A. S. Chowdhury, in the early 1970s.[36] They drafted a constitution for Bangladesh, the former East Pakistan, as it was by bloody rebellion achieving independence from the federation with West Pakistan. Abu Sayeed Chowdhury, the first President of Bangladesh, said of the chapter on individual rights in the Bangladesh Constitution:

> A study of these rights would at once make it clear that in their formulation, Magna Carta (1215), the Petition of Right (1628), the Bill of Rights (1689), and the Constitution of the United States of America, together with its amendments, were kept in mind. It is in this part of the Constitution that the full benefit of the written Constitution of the United States was taken as a model, and in fact, in dealing with these provisions the courts of Bangladesh freely refer to the judicial pronouncements of the Superior Courts of Britain, America and the Commonwealth countries.[37]

For former British territories such as Bangladesh, Sri Lanka, Malaysia, and Singapore, India has been an important source of judicial doctrine in constitutional law. The American influence on India's Constitution of 1950 was important, but on others it was more indirect and received through an Indian filter.[38] In the long drafting process leading to the Constitution of India, leaders in the Constituent Assembly consulted American experience extensively on such issues as federalism, judicial review, and individual rights. "Sir B. N. Rau, the Constitutional Adviser to the Constituent Assembly, and Sir Alladi Krishnaswamy Ayyar, one of the ablest and most respected lawyer members of the various committees set up by the Assembly, frequently relied on the Constitution of the United States."[39] Rau, in addition, had substantial discussions in the United States with President Harry Truman, American judges Felix Frankfurter and Learned Hand, and distinguished constitutional lawyers.[40] He cited among other documents the Articles of Confederation and the opinion of Chief Justice John Marshall in *McCulloch v. Maryland*.[41]

The Indian Constitution also presents a fascinating example of indirect American influence. After extended debate, Article 21 of the Indian basic law incorporated wording on procedural rights taken from Article 31 of the 1947 Constitution of Japan, so heavily influenced by American authorities: "No person shall be deprived of his life or personal property *except according to procedure established by law*" (phrasing from Japan italicized).[42] Although Indian jurists have looked most, of course, to their own vast store of accumulated case law, Indian courts by the time of this writing had cited American judicial precedents in about 1,000 cases since 1950.[43]

East Asia

In East Asia, the American presence was more substantial than in South or Southeast Asia (with the exception of the Philippines). Beginning in the mid-nineteenth century, American missionaries and teachers brought their ideas of democracy, law, and constitutionalism along with Christianity.[44] But the West imposed relations of inequality under its treaty law and virtually required, as one condition for regaining full national independence, the westernization of East Asian legal systems. Only Japan had achieved independence by 1900 or indeed before 1945.

China, with the first unequal treaties of the 1840s, began a century of suffering and searching for independence and new forms of government. In 1912, the Republic of China formally replaced the ancient monarchy. But regional warlords and the Nationalist Party–Communist Party civil war combined with the 1937–45 conflict with Japan to deny China peace and unity until the establishment of the People's Republic of China in 1949. Some early twentieth-century Chinese reformers thought their modern government should be modeled on the United States. There was serious talk into the 1920s of "united autonomous provinces" with a federalism analogous to that of America, but these leaders lacked the political and military power to govern.[45]

Until his death in 1925, Dr. Sun Yat-sen with his Nationalist Party (*Kuomintang*, KMT) advocated "Three Principles of the People" (nationalism, democracy, and the people's livelihood) which were compared to Lincoln's "government of the people, by the people and for the people," with which Sun was familiar.[46] Sun drew on Chinese as well as American and other traditions in developing his view of a "five-power government" (executive, legislative, judicial, impeachment, and the power to administer the civil service examinations) and "four powers of the people" (election, recall, initiative, referendum). He believed that after achieving independence and internal stability and after a period of tutelage, liberty and democracy should be extended to the people. Dr. Sun's views have remained the official ideology on Taiwan; they have seemed susceptible to development along lines of constitutional democracy, once martial law and one-party KMT rule was discarded.[47]

China, like other Asian countries, has accepted documentary constitutionalism, but one must read the Constitution of the People's Republic of China in conjunction with the rules of the Chinese Communist Party for a general grasp of state principles. For example, while the preamble of the 1982 Constitution extolled the primacy of "the leadership of the community party of China and the guidance of Marxism-Leninism and Mao Zedong Thought,"[48] Article 2 proclaimed "All power in the People's Republic of China belongs to the people."[49] China also illustrated most dramatically the critical role of legal development as a condition for constitutionalist government, even should China substantially modify its ideology in that direction. One reason for the nonconstitutionalist thrust of Chinese government was the severely atrophied state of law and legal institutions, especially after the disruptions of the Great Proletarian Cultural Revolution (1966–76).[50] After years of antilegal turmoil, China labored hard and systematically to build the legal infrastructure essential to government based on reasonably predictable law. In the process towards its first complete modern legal system, China has, for example, developed new penal codes establishing new rights, but, even assuming government intent to fully implement such codes, the legal professionals necessary for the task could not emerge in adequate numbers from educational institutions for many years. Each year in the 1980s, many thousands of Chinese students have come to American institutions, usually for training in the sciences and technology, but only a few in law. Such exchanges may not have a great effect on official thinking for some time, but they came at a time of seminal change and development in Chinese law and government and during a period of unprecedented access to America's constitutional experience.

The history of American influence on Korean constitutionalism culminated in the three-year occupation (1945–48), the massive United States participation in the United Nations defense of South Korea in the Korean War, and the subsequent direct American involvement in Korea's efforts at defence and at democratic constitutionalism. After Japan's annexation of Korea in 1910, the Korean movement for independence often combined nationalist preoccupations with American notions of constitutionalism and Christianity. A psychic dependence on American support for constitutional democracy in Korea developed then before World War II.[51] Christian political leaders such as Philip Jaisohn and Syngman Rhee were educated in the United States, while Americans founded churches, public health facilities, and schools in Korea. In response to Woodrow Wilson's call for self-determination for all peoples, the Koreans launched the March First Movement of 1919. This movement consisted of a prolonged series of peaceful nationwide demonstrations still commemorated annually as a pivotal event of modern national politics. An eloquent Korean Declaration of Independence called for freedom and equality in words echoing the American Declaration of Independence. It was only with the 1945 defeat of Japan, however, that Korea's "Liberation" finally came. But the joy of independence was cut short by the tragic division of the country after 1,200 years as a unified state with a homogeneous culture. Nevertheless, in South Korea the ideas of Christianity, human rights, and democracy from America have continued to be joined together in special nationalist legitimacy.[52]

From 1945 to 1948, USAMGIK (U.S. Military Government in Korea) ruled the South directly through ordinances, while the Soviet Union controlled the North through Kim Il-sung. In South Korea, five constitutions since independence (1948, 1960, 1962, 1972, and 1980) have not resolved an almost schizophrenic tension between authoritarianism and democratic constitutionalism. This situation was exacerbated by a persistent need for constant combat readiness against the North.[53] The Korean War only hardened the division and the determination to end it by "reunification," but Korea continued to remain divided.

The American Occupation led by Lt. General John R. Hodge had four goals: to remove the Japanese, to prepare the Koreans for self-government, to rebuild the economy, and to establish an effective democratic government. Support for constitutional democracy in Korea has remained basic to general American foreign policy ever since, but, in fact, United States influence over Korea's constitutional fate has been limited. Occupation efforts at democratic reform were inhibited by two factors: (1) the assumption that, unlike Japan, Korea was a liberated ally and therefore had to bear the onus for creating a new democracy, however impossible that task might be under the circumstances; and (2) the lack of planning, personnel, knowledge, and political stability, and the absence of a unified and compliant populace and a preexisting indigenous government.

The Japanese had left behind a developed but oppressive legal system, very few Koreans with administrative experience, and a large constabulary they had trained. The Koreans identified the 10,000 military and civilian police more with the hated Japanese than with credible nationalism. But the American military government came to rely upon them heavily for information and political advice. A severe shortage of legal professionals further exacerbated the difficulties of developing a coherent tradition of rights protection and constitutional government under law. "In 1945, only eight out of 120 prosecutors, 46 out of 235 judges and an estimated 195 qualified lawyers in the South were Korean. Only one of the lawyers had non-Japanese training."[54] Although most law kept in force by the Occupation was of Japanese origin, USAMGIK never had the services of an American specialist on Japanese law. Not one Korean law specialist existed in the West. USAMGIK did attempt, but with only limited success, to establish habeas corpus and other rights; but the inherited Korean bias favored officialdom, not the individual.[55] Tscholsu Kim, a leading constitutional lawyer, wrote:

> Probably the most significant measure taken by the U.S. Military Administration for Korean civil rights was "The Ordinance on the Rights of the Korean People" issued by General Hodge on April 7, 1948. The Ordinance consisted of twelve Articles guaranteeing the freedoms of religion, assembly and association, expression and publication, and the rights to legal counsel, to speedy and fair trial, and to equal protection under the law. It also prohibited torture and deprivation of freedom or property without due process of law. These precious principles were obviously derived from the basic doctrines of the Constitution of the United States... [and had] a consequential impact on the political leaders of Korea who were then preparing the nation for independence.[56]

Americans had very little to do with the drafting of the 1948 Constitution of the Republic—the so-called First Republic—but gave essential backing to the autonomy of the process. The Constitution Drafting Committee lacked much expertise, so it relied heavily on Professor Chin-o Yu, a renowned scholar. Yu looked to European rather than to American law and constitutions for guidance, but found the above-mentioned Ordinance very helpful when drafting provisions for individual rights.[57] The constitution established a strong president and many individual rights, but Syngman Rhee's increasingly dictatorial government led to his and its demise in 1960.

The 1960 Constitution of the Second Republic, written without notable American influence, reestablished constitutional democracy, but was soon replaced by military leadership in 1961. The Third Republic's Constitution (1962–72) was generally based upon American constitutional principles, with a strong presidency, separation of powers, individual rights, and judicial review. However, President Chung-hee Park, like Rhee before him, tried to perpetuate himself in office by constitutional amendments and became increasingly authoritarian. After Park's assassination in 1979, his 1972 *Yushin* (Revitalization) Constitution was discarded. The military government of President Doo-hwan Chun prepared the 1980 Constitution of the Fifth Republic, which restricted the President to one seven-year term but retained the *Yushin* system's reliance on an electoral college of thousands to elect the President. The opposition New Democratic Party and student organizations continued demands to restore direct popular election of the president and in 1986 the Sixth Republic Constitution was agreed to. No other state theory seems to compete for legitimacy in South Korea with democratic constitutionalism; fluctuations between respect for that ideal in practice and nonconstitutionalism have seemed characteristic over the decades.[58]

During the past forty years, the influence of American constitutionalism in Korea has existed within an unusual, sometimes sticky relationship of particularistic mutual dependency analogous to the United States–Philippine relationship.[59] Rightly or wrongly, many Koreans and Americans have felt that the United States has had unique international rights and duties with respect to Korea's internal affairs, thereby making it appropriate for America to be even more involved in the promotion of constitutionalism and rights in Korea. In the case of both Korea and the Philippines, military security, political stability, and economic development have vied with democratic constitutionalism for official attention. Torture and suppression of free speech have occurred. No president has yet come to office by peaceful transfer of power under law. Many argue that repression, imposed spasmodically, has diminished rather than enhanced Korea's security and economic needs. Unfortunately, official and private American pressure on the side of constitutional continuity and individual rights has been fitful and operative policy inconsistent.

At times, American congressmen and private organizations have criticized anticonstitutional behavior in Korea.[60] Occasionally, the American government has made aid conditional upon evidence of respect for human rights.[61] American occupation of Japan indirectly influenced Korea, when Korea adapted Japanese laws formulated during this period in Japanese history.[62] Education and research in the United States and Korea have increased understanding of the American constitutional system.[63] Korean children are taught democratic constitutionalism in the schools. Thousands of Korean students, professors, and administrative personnel in fields relevant to the implementation of constitutionalism have come to America for higher education. Some of these people, while retaining influential pro-democratic contacts in Korea, have chosen to teach or do other work in the United States.

In sum, since 1945, Americans and Koreans have shared the values of democratic constitutionalism in many contexts: the writing of the first Constitution with Occupation backing; the consultation with American constitutional experience at the time of the third Constitution and in the 1980s; interaction in education, economic aid missions, and trade negotiations; shared research projects; military cooperation; Christian church activities; and diplomatic affairs. Although these many contacts appear to be impressive, the quality of America's influence in constitutional matters might be better demonstrated if the United States were not so deeply enmeshed with South Korean governments for whom military security against North Korea has priority over the needs and rights of their own people.

THE AMERICAN OCCUPATION AND DEMOCRATIC CONSTITUTIONALISM IN JAPAN

In September 1945, when the Allied Occupation began, Japan had just suffered the worst defeat in its long history and was numb with devastation. The American-dominated Occupation in late 1945 and 1946 began an unpredictable and profound process of institutionalizing a revolution which set Japan on a course of democratic constitutionalism.[64] Within a broader perspective, this effort may have represented the most intense and significant instance in American history of a decisive extension of United States governance into a foreign land. The Occupation military government was headed by General Douglas MacArthur, who ruled indirectly through administrative personnel of the Japanese government and the emerging postwar political leaders. Guidelines were provided by Washington and the Potsdam Declaration, and Occupation directives were implemented by Japanese ordinances and laws.[65]

In the fall of 1945, MacArthur ordered the Japanese government to repeal repressive laws, to open the political system, to encourage unions, to give women suffrage, and to draft recommendations for a revision of the Meiji Constitution of 1889. MacArthur found the changes suggested in the "Matsumoto Draft" Constitution of February 1, 1946, to be inadequate. He entrusted the preparation of another draft constitution to the Occupation's Government Section, headed by his confidant General Courtney Whitney. Only three requirements were imposed on Whitney: (1) retain the emperor system, but make it subject to the people; (2) include a renunciation of Japan's right of international belligerency; and (3) eliminate "feudalism" and aristocracy.

The principal American authors of Japan's Constitution deserve to be much more widely known. Charles L. Kades, the Deputy Chief, formed a steering committee with two other lawyers—Alfred R. Hussey and Milo E. Powell—to oversee and participate in small committees which were set up to draft provisions on different subjects. Neither the members of the steering committee nor those who assisted them on the smaller committees were specialists in American constitutional law, let alone knowledgeable on Japanese public law. In their deliberations they had access only to a 1939 compendium of world constitutions found at a university, but not to a library with materials on the constitutional law or background of the United States and other countries. Far more important as sources for the Constitution of Japan were the convictions of the drafters and their memories of Western and American politics, law, and thought.

The product of this historic effort was presented to a shocked Japanese government on February 13, 1946. The steering committee members, especially Kades, were the principal authors:

> They, individually and collectively, wrote many of the provisions of the draft and rewrote, revised, or vetoed most of the provisions drawn up by their colleagues on the legislative, executive, judiciary, civil rights, local government, and finance committees into which the staff were divided.[66]

The Japanese government accepted the inevitable and joined vigorously in negotiations to refine the document. They employed such able people in the Cabinet Bureau as Toshio Irie (Supreme Court Justice, 1952–70) and Tatsuo Sato (later head of the National Personnel Authority). The resultant draft Constitution of Japan, with the blessing of Emperor Hirohito, was made public in English and Japanese on March 6, 1946. Further modifications were made by the Japanese Diet, and the new Constitution of Japan was promulgated on November 3, 1946, and went into effect May 3, 1947.

A constitution may enjoy the broad support of the people and must be implemented by laws, institutions, and official actions. United States influence continued as Americans and Japanese worked together to remake law to fit the new order. In this regard, perhaps Alfred Oppler, a refugee German judge with expertise in German law on which much of Japan's system had been based, was most important:

> Oppler will long be remembered for his revision of the Japanese codes of law along democratic lines. It was he who brought about the sweeping reforms of the Civil, Criminal, and Procedural Codes and the enactment of the Court Organization Law, innovations that breathed life into the new constitution. . . .[67]

Others were Thomas Blakemore of Oklahoma, then America's only trained specialist in Japanese law; Kurt Steiner, later of Stanford University; Daniel Imbodden, who worked with the press; and, of course, Charles Kades. Contrary to popular opinion, these men went beyond American sources: "[T]he changes we brought about in close cooperation with the Japanese legal world were not blindly copied from Anglo-Saxon jurisprudence, but were the fruit of an endeavor to combine the best features of both the continental and the Anglo-Saxon systems."[68] The Occupation officials counterbalanced massive intervention with cooperative interaction with the Japanese.

Japanese and American lawyers joined forces to inaugurate the Japan Civil Liberties Union in 1947, when MacArthur invited Roger Baldwin of the American Civil Liberties Union to Japan.[69] In 1950, Oppler and Kades brought five Japanese Supreme Court Justices to the United States to introduce them to the judicial practices of the Supreme Court. Oppler's mention on another occasion of America's new civil liberties unit in the Justice Department led Yoshio Suzuki, Steiner, and others to establish in 1948 the still-successful system of Civil Liberties Commissioners (*Jinken Yogo Iin*, literally "human rights protectors").[70] As of 1985, some 11,500 carefully selected and unpaid law commissioners, with no police powers, were assisting hundreds of thousands of citizens each year at the grass-roots level, quickly, cheaply, and respectfully.

American influence was decisive in determining the main features of Japan's Constitution: popular sovereignty; a powerless dynastic emperor; a bicameral Diet composed of a dominant House of Representatives and a House of Councillors; a Prime Minister and Cabinet who exercise collectively the executive power but are responsible to the Diet; a unitary national state, but with provision for some local autonomy and democratically elected local governments; a Supreme Court and other courts with full administrative independence and powers of judicial review; and a wide range of enforceable individual rights (Chapter 3, Articles 11 to 40).[71] The "no-war" clause of Article 9 was the main reason why Japan has had over forty years of unbroken peace in her international relations, why militarists have been excluded from political power, and why Japan's armament has been carefully limited.[72]

The catalyst provided by Occupation officials gave lasting legitimacy to a democratic constitutionalism and peaceful internationalism. Japan's Constitution has become one of the oldest and most popular in the world, because it has fit the country's politico-legal culture, national needs, and popular desires, and because many Japanese have been vigilant in its defence. The Japanese people and government deserve most of the credit for the success of constitutional democracy in Japan, and this point may need emphasis lest American readers be tempted to slip into a chauvinistic American stance. On the other hand, it seems improbable that Japan would have evolved easily into a constitutional democracy if Occupation officials had stood aside, as they did in South Korea. The minority "revisionist" view in Japan that American origins have somehow tarnished the Constitution with a foreign tinge ignores the overwhelming support the document has continued to enjoy. American authorities, it is true, did bypass the preferences of some in positions of power in deference to the desires of the general citizenry. The revisionists were correct, however, in stressing the extraordinary, indeed unprecedented, American influence on the Japanese Constitution.

In two related areas, America's living constitution seems to have been very important to Japan: human rights and judicial power. The 1947 Constitution embodied an explication of American rights in the period right after the Great Depression, New Deal, and World War II, as such rights were understood by Charles Kades and other "Occupationnaires." It was only later that some of these rights were included in such documents as the United Nations Declaration of Universal Human Rights of 1948. In general terms, Articles 11 to 13 and 97 of the Constitution listed the rights of Japanese citizens as "eternal and inviolate," as "fundamental human rights," and that "life, liberty and the pursuit of happiness," would in general "be the supreme consideration in legislation and in other governmental affairs.[73] Specifically, Article 14 banned "discrimination in political, economic, or social relations because of race, creed, sex, social status, or family origin," while Article 24 recognized the equal marriage rights of women. Although some problems remain regarding the status of women in society, women's rights in Japan have improved dramatically since 1945.

Under Article 29, the right to hold and use property was made subject to "the public welfare," that is, to public policy for such purposes as implementing Article 25 or 26. Article 25 recognized a right defensible in court "to maintain the minimum standards of wholesome and cultured living," and to "social welfare and security." All citizens, in addition, have a constitutional right to free education, and parents or guardians have a duty to see that this right is exercised (Article 26).

Workers have rights, which must be implemented by laws, to reasonable standards for "wages, hours, rest and other working conditions" (Article 27) and the rights "to organize and to bargain and act collectively" (Article 28). All persons have a right to vote by secret ballot; and discrimination on various grounds, such as set forth in Article 14, and interfering with Diet candidacy or voting is prohibited (Articles 15, 44).

Article 31 of the Constitution introduces a panoply of procedural rights: "No person shall be deprived of life or liberty, nor shall any other criminal penalty be imposed, except according to procedure established by law." In this area of individual rights (as in most others), Japan's record has been good, because of the highly professional judges, prosecutors, and police.[74]

"The rights and freedoms of the spirit," as scholars call them, have been crucial to a formerly oppressed people: all forms of freedom of expression are guaranteed (Article 21), as are freedoms of thought, conscience (Article 19), religion (Article 20), and professional academic activities (Article 23).[75]

Chapter 6 established for the first time a judiciary under the administrative control of the Supreme Court. The judiciary has the "whole" and "final judicial power" (Article 76) and the right "to determine the constitutionality of any law, order, regulation or official act" (Article 81). Interestingly, it was the Japanese, not the American, participants in the constitution-drafting process who insisted more on giving the bench full rather than partial powers of judicial review.[76]

Japan has, of course, applied general legal and constitutional principles in keeping with its own traditions and European practices. But it is incontestable that American influence helped to establish the rights, laws, governmental machinery, and the new ethos that supported continuation of the constitutional revolution of freedom.

Since independence in 1952, at least six other kinds of American constitutional influence were evident: (1) consultation within Japan or the United States of American experience on constitutional issues by Japanese scholars, judges, prosecutors, lawyers, and students;[77] (2) the inclusion of references to American judicial and scholarly work in Japanese law textbooks, treatises, and law journals;[78] (3) the avoidance of any recommendations for amendment by the Commission on the Constitution, and the move towards reliance on judicial refinement of doctrine based on the American model;[79] (4) the Japanese American Society for Legal Studies, which has further institutionalized study of each other's law by Japanese and Americans, including influential judges, scholars, lawyers, and prosecutors;[80] (5) the consultation by Japanese judges of American constitutional precedents and related Japanese and American commentaries, and the use of testimony by Japanese specialists on

American constitutional law;[81] and (6) collaborative research by American and Japanese legal scholars on constitutional issues.[82]

In framing Japan's Constitution, the United States exercised perhaps its greatest postwar influence upon any foreign constitution. The American drafters were not constitutional lawyers: they were men of considerable ability and clarity of purpose who seized the opportunity presented by a unique moment in cross-cultural history. They were able to work with a remarkably able and cooperative group of Japanese and to help initiate a far-reaching revolution of law and constitution.

CONCLUSION

America's influence on constitutionalism and democratic constitutionalism in Asia has taken many shapes and forms. Sometimes it has been through consultations, when Asian constitutions have been written, revised, or amended. In other instances, it has been through the dissemination of American constitutional values by means of education, cultural exchanges, or the mass media. In yet other cases, it has been through the adoption of judicial review powers or positions taken by American courts, legal scholars, or lawyers. The American commitment to civil liberties, to orderly processes of dispute resolution, and to the peaceful transfer of political leadership has impressed many Asian constitutionalists. Less consonant with Asian values and with their high expectation of American commitment to constitutionalism and human rights has been the record of the United States with respect to racial equality, socioeconomic fairness, and certain aspects of criminal justice.

Asia with its astonishing diversity, cultural richness, and different political systems has moved gradually toward an array of governments more committed to constitutionalism and often to democratic constitutionalism. The region has become a rewarding source for comparative perspectives on approaches to state theories and practices. One would hope that if the United States celebrates its constitutional tricentennial, it will be joined by many Asian countries celebrating their constitutions and that Americans will have enriched their own heritage by a greater and more sensitive understanding of other traditions of constitutional democracy. For that to come to pass, Americans, along with Asian counterparts, will have to adopt a broadly internationalist and interdisciplinary approach to constitutional law. Both will have to eschew the following view expressed by a distinguished Western jurist in Asia: "The Constitution is primarily to be interpreted within its four walls, and not in the light of analogies drawn from other countries. . . ."[83]

It is rather by a cross-cultural approach to the great constitutional issues of the world that law and civilization will move more constructively into the future.

NOTES

Thanks are due to George A. Billias and Walter F. Murphy for their very helpful comments on an earlier draft.

1. For background on Asia and the United States, see Lawrence Ward Beer, ed., *Constitutionalism in Asia: Asian Views of the American Influence* (Berkeley: University of California Press, 1979), chap. 1; and Selig Harrison, *The Widening Gulf: Asian Nationalism and American Policy* (New York: Free Press, 1978). For current information on each Asian country, see *Asian Survey* (University of California Press), the annual January and February issues, and the *Asia Yearbook* (*Far Eastern Economic Review*, Hong Kong). On Asian law, see the *Pacific Basin Law Journal* (UCLA Law School, Los Angeles), *Lawasia* (Law Association for Asia and the Western Pacific, Sydney, Australia), and *Law in Japan* (Japanese American Society for Legal Studies, Law School, University of Washington).

2. T. K. K. Iyer, a review of Beer, *Constitutionalism*, in *Malaya Law Review* 23 (1981): 210–11.

3. On the various law traditions, see John Henry Merryman, *The Civil Law Tradition* (Stanford: Stanford University Press, 1969); Mary Ann Glendon, Michael Wallace Gordon, and Christopher Osakwe, *Comparative Legal Traditions* (St. Paul: West Publishing Co., 1982); M. B. Hooker, *Islamic Law in Southeast Asia* (Singapore: Oxford University Press, 1984), and *Legal Pluralism: An Introduction to Colonial and neo-Colonial Laws* (Oxford: Clarendon Press, 1975).

4. John K. Fairbanks, Edwin O. Reischauer, and Albert Craig, *East Asia: Tradition and Transformation* (Boston: Houghton-Mifflin, 1978).

5. The latest revision dates were provided by Albert P. Blaustein, *Constitutions of the Countries of the World*, 17 vols. (Dobbs Ferry, N.Y.: Oceana Publications, 1986). On problems of nation building in diverse settings, see Crawford Young, *The Politics of Cultural Pluralism* (Madison: University of Wisconsin Press, 1974); Hooker, *Legal Pluralism*; Lucian Pye, *Asian Power and Politics* (Cambridge: Harvard University Press, 1985); and R. N. Spann, ed., *Constitutionalism in Asia* (Bombay: Asia Publishing House, 1963).

6. Blaustein, *Constitutions*; Beer, *Constitutionalism*; and Jagdish Lal, *The Constitution of India as Amended by the Forty-Second Amendment* (Delhi: Delhi Law House, 1977). The years these nations became independent after World War II were: Japan, 1952; China, 1945; India, 1947; and Indonesia, 1949.

7. Lawrence Ward Beer, *Freedom of Expression in Japan: A Study in Comparative Law, Politics, and Society* (Tokyo & New York: Kodansha International and Harper & Row, 1985), chap. 1; and Walter F. Murphy, "An Ordering of Constitutional Values," *Southern California Law Review* 53 (1980): 703–60.

8. I. W. Mabbett, ed., *Patterns of Kingship and Authority in Traditional Asia* (London: Croom Helm, 1985; and James C. Hsiung, ed., *Human Rights in East Asia* (New York: Paragon House Publishers, 1986).

9. Hooker, *Legal Pluralism* and *Islamic Law in Southeast Asia*; Beer, *Constitu-*

tionalism; and Majik Khadduri, *The Islamic Conception of Justice* (Baltimore: Johns Hopkins University Press, 1985).

10. I. W. Mabbett, *Patterns of Kingship*; Robert Heine-Geldern, *Conceptions of State and Kinship in Southeast Asia*, Data Paper no. 18, Southeast Asia Program (Ithaca, N.Y.: Cornell University, April 1976); Hooker, *Legal Pluralism*; and Joseph A. L. Cooray, *Constitutional and Administrative Law of Sri Lanka (Ceylon)* (Colombo: Hansa Publishers, 1973), 563.

11. Beer, *Freedom*, chap. 2.

12. Beer, *Constitutionalism*, chap. 1.

13. Ibid., 16 and passim.

14. Ibid., passim; Clark D. Neher, *Politics in Southeast Asia* (Cambridge: Schenkman Publishing Co., 1981); and David Morell and Chai-anan Samudvanija, *Political Conflict in Thailand* (Cambridge: Oelgeschlager, Gunn, & Hain, 1982).

15. *The Japan Times*, October 17, 1986, and discussions with sources in Japan. Jyh-pain Fa, *A Comparative Study of Judicial Review under Nationalist Chinese and American Constitutional Law, OP/RCAS*, no. 4, University of Maryland Law School, 1980.

16. Lawrence W. Beer, "Constitutional Revolution in Japanese Law, Society, and Politics," *Modern Asian Studies* 16 (1982): 33–40.

17. Beer, *Constitutionalism*, 18; and Oemar Seno Adji, "An Indonesian Perspective on the American Constitutional Influence," in Beer, *Constitutionalism*, 102–5.

18. Ibid.; and Tun Mohamed Suffian, H. R. Lee, and F. A. Rindale, eds., *The Constitution of Malaysia, 1957–1977* (Kuala Lumpur: Oxford University Press, 1978), 101–122.

19. Adji, "An Indonesian Perspective," 102; and Suffian et al., 163–207.

20. Tun Mohamed Suffian, "The Malaysian Constitution and the United States Constitution," in Beer, *Constitutionalism*, 136.

21. P. K. Tripathi, "Perspectives on the American Constitutional Influence on the Constitution of India," in Beer, *Constitutionalism*, 62–63.

22. Ibid., 57–71.

23. Ibid., 67.

24. Beer, *Constitutionalism*, 17; and Tripathi, "Perspectives," 60–62.

25. Article 50 in Lal, *The Constitution of India*, 173.

26. Ivo D. Duchacek, *Power Maps: Comparative Politics of Constitutionalism* (Santa Barbara: ABC Clio Press, 1973).

27. Adam Malik, *In the Service of the Republic* (Jakarta: Gunung Agung, 1980), 8–9, 129.

28. M. Yamin, as quoted in Adji, "An Indonesian Perspective," 104.

29. *The Constitution of the Republic of Indonesia* and "Elucidation of the Constitution" (1945 and 1959), provided by the Pancasila Council, Jakarta, Indonesia, 1984; and Adji, "An Indonesian Perspective," 103–4.

30. James L. Magaver, "Editorial Note," 141–43 and Enrique M. Fernando, "The American Constitutional Impact on the Philippine Legal System," 144–48, in Beer, *Constitutionalism*; and Roberto Regala, *Making the Constitution Responsive to Economic and Social Problems*, Philippine Constitution Association, May 14, 1969.

31. On American problems regarding rights, see Robert Pringle, *Indonesia and the Philippines* (New York: Columbia University Press, 1980), 89; Enrique M. Fernando, *Reflections on the Revised Constitution* (Manila: Aklatan Pretla, 1973); William J. Butler, John P. Humphrey, and G. E. Bisson, *The Decline of Democracy in the Philippines* (Geneva: International Commission of Jurists, 1977); Emma Quisumbing-Fernando, *Philippine Constitutional Law* (Manila: CLPCI, 1984); Purificacion V. Quisumbing, ed., *The New Constitution and Human Rights* (Quezon City: University of Philippines Law Center, 1979); and Harry M. Scoble and Laurie S. Wiseberg, eds., *Access to Justice* (London: Zed Books, 1985), 101–5.

32. On the Philippines, see Pye, *Asian Power and Politics*, and Neher, *Politics in Southeast Asia*. On the 1986 developments, see *New York Times*, *Christian Science Monitor*, *Asiaweek* (Hong Kong), and *Far Eastern Economic Review* (Hong Kong), from February through June 1986. On the proposed Constitution, *Asahi Shimbun*, October 13, 1986, and *The Japan Times*, October 14 and 17, 1986.

33. Cooray, *Law of Sri Lanka*, 509–11. The one exception, based on the importance of divisions between the majority Sinhalese and the Tamils, was Section 23(2) which "prohibited legislation infringing religious freedom or discriminating against persons of any community or religion." Ibid.

34. Discussion with C. G. Weeramantry of Monash University, Australia, past Justice of the Supreme Court of Sri Lanka, in March 1985.

35. Cooray, *Law of Sri Lanka*, 510–11.

36. Albert P. Blaustein, "The United States Constitution: A Model in Nation Building," *National Forum* (Fall 1984): 17, and the more detailed manuscript version.

37. Mr. Justice Abu Sayeed Chowdhury, "The Bangladesh Constitution in American Perspective," in Beer, *Constitutionalism*, 30.

38. Even where British antecedents were primary, as in Malaysia, legal scholars commonly knew of an American alternative view on an issue or of the comments of jurists such as Oliver Wendell Holmes. For examples of references in a multi-authored Asian book, see Suffian et al., 10, 31, 34, 37, 126, 136, 177, 181. Philippine constitution writings and court decisions have been replete with references to the American experience.

39. Tripathi, "Perspectives," 64.

40. Ibid., 64–71.

41. Ibid., 64–65.

42. Ibid., 85.

43. Communication from George Gadbois, University of Kentucky, 1984; Granville Austin, *The Indian Constitution: Cornerstone of a Nation* (London: Oxford University Press, 1966); and Marc Galanter, *Competing Equalities* (Berkeley: University of California Press, 1984), 522–67.

44. Fairbanks, *East Asia*, 435–647, 682–894; and James C. Thompson, Jr., Peter W. Stanley, and John Curtis Perry, *Sentimental Imperialists: The American Experience in East Asia* (New York: Harper and Row, 1981).

45. Beer, *Constitutionalism*, 6–7; and Herbert N. P. Ma, "American Influence on the Formation of the Constitution and Constitutional Law of the Republic of China," in Beer, *Constitutionalism*, 39–55.

46. Ma, "Influence," 42–50; Ch'ien Tuan-sheng, *The Government and Politics*

of China, 1912–1949 (Stanford: Stanford University Press, 1970); and Fairbanks, *East Asia*, 726–807.

47. On the state of constitutionalism on Taiwan, see Hsiung, ed., *Human Rights in East Asia*, 93–102; and the annual January articles on Taiwan in *Asian Survey*.

48. *The Constitution of the People's Republic of China*, adopted December 4, 1982 (Beijing: Foreign Language Press, 1983), 3–11.

49. Ibid., 11. See Andrew J. Nathan, *Chinese Democracy* (New York: Alfred A. Knopf, 1985).

50. William C. Jones, "The Constitution of the People's Republic of China," *Washington University Law Quarterly* 63 (1986): 707–35; and James P. Brady, *Justice and Politics in People's China* (New York: Academic Press, 1982), 41–45.

51. Chong-sik Lee, *The Politics of Korean Nationalism* (Berkeley: University of California Press, 1975), 167, 277–78 and passim.

52. Ibid.; Gregory Henderson, *Korea: The Politics of the Vortex* (Cambridge: Harvard University Press, 1968), 80–86; Bruce Cumings, *The Two Koreas*, Headline Series, no. 269, 1984, Foreign Policy Association; and Pyong-ho Park et al., *Modernization and Its Impact upon Korean Law* (Berkeley: Institute of East Asian Studies, 1981). For the texts of South Korean constitutions, see Se-jin Kim and Chang-hyun Cho, *Government and Politics in Korea* (Silver Springs, Maryland: Institute of Korean Affairs, 1972), 275, as amended through 1969; *Journal of Korean Affairs*, April 1973, 39, the *Yushin* Constitution; and *The Korea Times*, Seoul, September 30, 1980. See also Bruce Cumings, ed., *Child of Conflict: The Korean-American Relationship, 1943–1953* (Seattle: University of Washington Press, 1983).

53. Henderson, *Korea*, and "Human Rights in South Korea, 1945–1953," in Edward Baker and William Shaw, eds., *Human Rights in Korea: Historical and Policy Perspectives*, forthcoming; and sources cited in supra, note 52.

54. Henderson, "Human Rights," 17.

55. Ibid., 28, 157–59; and Donald MacDonald, *Korea and the Ballot: the International Dimension in Korean Political Development as Seen in Elections*, Ph.D. dissertation, George Washington University, 1977, 225.

56. Tscholsu Kim, "The Influence of the U.S. Constitution on the Korean Constitution," *Seoul Law Journal* 26 (1985) (in Korean; trans. San Don Lee).

57. Ibid.

58. Sugwon Kang, "Thoughts on the 'Korean Style of Democracy,' " *Journal of Korean Affairs* (April 1974): 26; Jahn-hae Yoo and Larry L. Wade, "A Study of Current Korean Political Culture: An Interpretive Perspective," *Journal of East Asian Affairs* (Seoul, 1981): 118–72; and L. L. Wade, "South Korean Political Culture: An Interpretation of Survey Data," *Journal of Korean Studies* 2 (1980): 1.

59. Pringle, *Indonesia and the Philippines*, 89.

60. See, for example, *Monthly Review of Korean Affairs* (Arlington, Virginia: Friends of the Korean People). Note also American media reports of Dae-jung Kim's return to Seoul from the United States in February 1985.

61. David C. Cole and Princeton N. Lyman, *Korean Development: The Interplay of Politics and Economics* (Cambridge: Harvard University Press, 1971), 59–62; and W. D. Reeve, *The Republic of Korea: A Political and Economic Study* (New York: Oxford University Press, 1963).

62. Hyong-bae Kim, "Labor Law in Korea," in Pyong-ho Pak et al., *Modernization*, 65; and Ki Yop Lim, "Development of Korean Labor Law and Practice," *Journal of Korean Affairs* (January 1976): 25.

63. MacDonald, *Korea and the Ballot*, 140–41. The semi-public Asia Foundation helped to establish the Korean Legal Center in Seoul, on behalf of improved legal publications and services. American specialists on Korea have often exemplified United States constitutional ideas in their dealings with Koreans.

64. Beer, *Freedom*, 37–46, 71–100; and Beer, "Revolution," 33–36.

65. Justin Williams, *Japan's Political Revolution under MacArthur* (Athens: University of Georgia Press, 1978), 108; SCAP, *Political Reorientation of Japan*, vol. 1 (Washington, D.C.: Government Printing Office, n.d. [1949]; and Dale Hellegers in *The Occupation of Japan: The Proceedings of a Seminar on the Occupation of Japan and Its Legacy to the Postwar World* (Norfolk: MacArthur Memorial, 1976), 11–15.

66. Williams, *Japan*, 39–42.

67. Ibid., 64–65.

68. Alfred Oppler, *Legal Reform in Occupied Japan: A Participant Looks Back* (Princeton: Princeton University Press, 1976), 71.

69. Ibid., 178–82.

70. Lawrence W. Beer, "Human Rights Commissioners (*Jinken Yogo Iin*) and Lay Protection of Human Rights in Japan," Occasional Paper no. 31 (October 1985), International Ombudsman Institute, Alberta, Canada.

71. Hiroshi Itoh and Lawrence W. Beer, *The Constitutional Case Law of Japan* (Seattle: University of Washington Press, 1978), 258–61.

72. Lawrence W. Beer, "Japan's Constitutional System and Its Judicial Interpretation," *Law in Japan* 17 (1984): 11–13. Article 9 reads:

> Aspiring sincerely to an international peace based on justice and order, the Japanese people forever renounce war as a sovereign right of the nation and the threat or use of force as a means of settling international disputes.
>
> . . . In order to accomplish the aim of the preceding paragraph, land, sea, and air forces, as well as other war potential, will never be maintained. The right of belligerency of the state will not be recognized. (Ibid., 258)

73. Ibid., 256–58. The "public welfare," the standard by which the exercise of rights may be limited under the Constitution, has been defined by the Supreme Court to mean maintenance of human rights and public order. *Japan v. Sugino*, 4 *KEISHU* 2012, 2014 (Sup. Ct., Grand Bench, 1950).

74. Beer, *Freedom*; David H. Bayley, *Forces of Order: Police Behavior in Japan and the United States* (Berkeley: University of California Press, 1976); and B. J. George, Jr., "Discretionary Authority of Public Prosecutors in Japan," *Law in Japan* 17 (1984): 42.

75. There is no state religion, but citizens were not free to disregard State Shinto, the prewar orthodoxy, before 1945, because it was excluded from the official definition of "religion" for which freedom was guaranteed. Recent right-wing politicians have adopted a similar stance, denying that official visits to (formerly State) Shinto shrines were "religious" in nature, but their view is accepted by very few constitutional lawyers.

76. David J. Danelski, "Judicial Review and Democracy in Japan," a paper

for the International Political Science Association meeting, Paris, July 1985, 1–6; Nobusige Ukai, "The Significance of the Reception of American Constitutional Institutions and Ideas in Japan," in Beer, *Constitutionalism*, 114–17; translated Supreme Court decisions have appeared in John M. Maki, *Court and Constitution in Japan: Selected Supreme Court Decisions, 1948–1960* (Seattle: University of Washington Press, 1964); and in Itoh and Beer, *Case Law*.

77. These comments are based on decades of interaction with Japanese legal professionals.

78. See, for example, such leading law journals as *Jurisuto* (Yuhikaku Publishing Co.), *Horitsu Jiho* (Nihon Hyoronsha), and the student-oriented *Hogaku Kyoshitsu* (Yuhikaku), all published in Tokyo.

79. Kenzo Takayanagi, "Appendix: Opinion on Some Constitutional Problems—the Rule of Law," in Dan Fenno Henderson, ed., *The Constitution of Japan: Its First Twenty Years, 1947–1967* (Seattle: University of Washington Press, 1968); and John M. Maki, *Japan's Commission on the Constitution: Its Final Report* (Seattle: University of Washington Press, 1980).

80. *Law in Japan* is available through the Asian Law Program, JB–20, University of Washington, Seattle, Washington.

81. Beer, *Freedom*, 325–26, and "Japan's Constitutional System," 26–27. Examples of influential court testimony by Japan's specialists on American constitutional law have included that of Masami Ito (now Justice Ito) in a case establishing the right of privacy in Japanese law, and that of Nobuyoshi Ashibe on behalf of a "less restrictive alternative" doctrine in a free speech case.

82. Examples include: the journal, *Law in Japan*; Henderson, *The Constitution of Japan*; Beer, *Freedom*, and the Japanese translation of *Constitutionalism* entitled *Ajia nokempo seido* (Gakuyo Shobo, 1981).

83. Suffian et al., 187.

Bibliographical Essay

The historiography dealing with the spread of American constitutionalism abroad represents a serious gap in the literature of American history in general and of comparative constitutional history in particular. Only about a dozen books and a host of articles touch upon this most important topic, but none treat the subject comprehensively in geographical terms nor in a systematic chronological manner. The dozen or so books, moreover, represent different disciplines—history, political science, and comparative constitutional law—and by approaching the subject from alternative perspectives often come to different conclusions.

Two approaches mark this brief overview of the literature. A short discussion of *what* has been written comes first—that is, the work itself is described and analyzed in short compass. An inquiry then follows, indicating *when* the work was written in order to place the piece within some kind of historiographical context.

The story commences with a significant historiographical controversy at the turn of the twentieth century between two European scholars—Georg Jellinek and Émile Doumergue. The two men debated what superficially appeared to be a narrow and technical question. Was it the declaration of rights in the first American state constitutions—especially that of Virginia on May 15, 1776 framed mainly by George Mason—that began the bill of rights tradition? Or was it the French Declaration of the Rights of Man and the Citizen of 1789 that marked its origins? What were involved were broader issues: was it America or France which was the forerunner of this great tradition in Western constitutionalism? Was natural law tradition the source of the rights of man, or were they derived separately from English common law and practices? Were the roots of this tradition secular, or did they rise from the struggle for religious liberty?

Jellinek, a German jurist, authored a widely known book, *Die Erklärung der Menschen und Bürgerrechte* in 1895, which advanced the argument that the French Declaration was not derived from Rousseau, but rather from the American state bills of rights. Jellinek contended further that the true origins of the rights of man could be traced to the struggle for religious liberty that began with the Agreement of the People in England in 1647 and culminated in the American colonies. The natural law tradition, he concluded, could not be considered an adequate explanation for the rights of man.[1]

Jellinek's book became the center of a heated debate. It sparked a response from a Frenchman, Émile Doumergue, who drew a direct line of descent of the rights of man from Calvin to the French Declaration. David G. Ritchie, on the other hand, in *Natural Rights*, came to a conclusion in 1903 quite independently of Jellinek that there was a religious influence involved in the struggle for the rights of man.[2]

The next set of writings came almost a half century later on the occasion of the sesquicentennial celebration of the Federal Constitution. To mark the 150th anniversary, Conyers Read, secretary of the American Historical Association, edited a volume in 1938 entitled, *The Constitution Reconsidered*. He demonstrated his awareness of the influence of the Federal Constitution abroad by labelling the third section in his book, "Repercussions of the Constitution Outside the United States." This volume included scattered essays sampling the influence of the American Constitution on Canada, South Africa, Latin America, the federal systems in the British empire, the Weimar Constitution of 1919, and in general terms within Europe from 1789 to 1815. The contributors included distinguished scholars from the fields of history, political science, and law: Geoffrey Bruun, Robert C. Binkley, Hajo Holborn, W. Menzies Whitelaw, Clarence H. Haring, C. P. Wright, and Cornelius W. de Kiewiet.[3]

Generally speaking, the contributors confined their focus almost exclusively to the Federal Constitution and, as a result, failed to find significant American influences in the foreign countries or specialized areas they studied. There were some exceptions. Whitelaw discovered that the American version of federalism had affected two British federal systems—the Canadian and Australian. In Latin America, Haring concluded that the Brazilian Constitution of 1889 followed closely the Federal Constitution of 1787. And in South Africa, de Kiewiet noted that the constitution-makers in three states—Natal, the Orange Free State, and the Transvaal—all had before them copies of the Federal Constitution.[4]

At about the same time—in 1939—John A. Hawgood, an English author, published *Modern Constitutions Since 1787*. Unlike the contributors to the Conyers Read volume, Hawgood did not focus on the Federal Constitution but summarized briefly the written constitutions of practically every country in the world. The value of his book lay in the comparisons Hawgood made between the Federal Constitution and the constitutions of the other great powers. Written on the eve of World War II, the book represented a defence of the democratic way of life against the threat of fascism and communism.[5]

On the eve of World War II, one of the scholars who eventually was to make a major contribution to the field, Carl J. Friedrich, began publishing works that touched upon the parameters of the problem of studying the spread of America's constitutional influence abroad. Born and educated in Germany, Friedrich came to the United States in the 1920s as a young man and wrote a significant study in 1932 on the thought of Johannes Althusius. A Dutch Calvinist political theorist, Althusius—who lived from the mid–1550s to the late 1630s—was the intellectual father of the modern conception of federalism and an advocate of popular sovereignty. Friedrich, who taught at Harvard, also wrote in 1937 a pioneering textbook on comparative government entitled *Constitutional Government and Politics*. In his work Friedrich resorted to a functional and topical analysis of the framework of constitutional government rather than a country-by-country approach. In 1967, when publishing his important monograph in the field, *The Impact of American Constitutionalism Abroad*, Friedrich employed the same technique.[6]

Friedrich began with the premise that the three main elements in American constitutionalism were presidentialism, federalism, and judicial review (though he restricted his discussion of the latter only as it related to human rights). Presidentialism, he noted, had been adopted mainly by some Latin American countries. He was quick to add, however, that they had changed the nature of the institution because they often failed to incorporate the checks and balances and separation of powers employed as safeguards against dictatorship in the American system. The American version of federalism, he concluded, was the constitutional feature imitated most by foreign countries. But again countries adapted the institutions to suit their needs as they sought to balance centralizing interests with local ones. Judicial review—with an enforcement of the Bill of Rights provided by courts when individuals believed their rights had been violated—was widely admired abroad, he noted. Friedrich observed, however, that this feature of American constitutionalism had been accepted only rarely in the rest of the world by the mid–1960s.[7]

Given as a series of lectures, Friedrich's book was a tour de force, a remarkable contribution, and remains one of the major landmarks in the field. The work revealed his commanding grasp of political theory, comparative constitutionalism, and European and American history. Because of his European background, his position as professor at both Harvard and the University of Heidelberg, and his penetrating mind, Friedrich was able to bring to bear an unusual mastery to his subject. Though his insights were original, the brevity imposed by the lecture format prevented him from developing any of his themes at great length or depth. Thus, the study is suggestive more than substantive and idiosyncratic rather than definitive.

Friedrich represented also a somewhat new phenomenon in the field of comparative constitutional history during the post–World War II period—that of the scholar-activist. Besides his teaching career, publications, and lectures, Friedrich was actually involved in the writing of constitutions. Between 1946 and 1949, he served as adviser to the American military governor in Germany and helped to frame the Bonn Constitution of 1949. He was also a constitutional adviser to Puerto Rico and contributed to the drafting of the Constitution of that Commonwealth adopted in 1952. And in the early 1950s, he held the post of constitutional adviser to the European Constituent Assembly. What was significant is that he helped to set an example for American scholars. Other constitutional scholars in the post–World War II era, as we shall see, served as constitutional advisers to foreign countries. In doing so, they often introduced features of the Federal Constitution in the documents they helped to prepare.

The second great landmark in the literature of the post–World War II era was Robert R. Palmer's magisterial two-volume work, *The Age of the Democratic Revolution*, published in 1959 and 1964. Palmer's study, of course, covered much more than comparative constitutional history. But in his historical synthesis—which argued that the whole of Western civilization was swept up in a single revolutionary movement stretching from the 1770s to the 1840s—Palmer perforce had to deal with constitutional reforms. A great history of this magnitude could hardly avoid dealing with political theory and constitutionalism.

Palmer's history characterized the democratic revolution that he found focal to the age from the 1770s to the European revolutions of 1848 as a series of upheavals with no single center. They represented assaults upon the forms of social stratification and upon the ideas of the possession of governments or positions of established power by privileged, closed, and self-perpetuating groups. Such attacks varied from place to place and country to country in the ancien régime in Europe as well as in America. In short, this revolutionary movement was international in character and crossed the Atlantic. The attacks culminated ultimately in the American, French, and Belgian revolutions in the period Palmer covered most closely from 1770 to 1800. Palmer's history, as far as constitutional changes are concerned, however, stopped at about the year 1800.

One of the main theses of Palmer's work was the revolutionary nature of the American Revolution. Among the truly radical and original constitutional features of the American Revolution, Palmer pointed out, was the introduction of the constituent constitutional convention. This innovation, in his eyes, ranked as America's most important contribution to the world in terms of political theory and practice. The concept of the constituent power of the people at work in a constitutional way was a radical idea which was destined to have worldwide implications.

Palmer's work stands, without doubt, as the most brilliant study of the expansion of American constitutionalism we have to date. The study, however, is confined primarily to Europe and North America and covers only the years down to 1800. Nevertheless, the sweep of its synthesis, the thoughtful analysis of ideas and institutions, and the careful qualification of his overall thesis make Palmer's work a model for other scholars on this subject to follow.[8]

The third landmark study in the postwar period was Richard B. Morris's *The Emerging Nations and the American Revolution*, published in 1970. Morris was concerned not only with the influence of the Revolution upon the emerging nations, but also with the constitutional developments that followed. The United States, he suggested, could serve as a model for emerging new states because of the following analogies: each of them had its declaration of independence, war of national liberation, and crisis of legitimacy. Morris cast his net wide and discussed developments in broad terms both in time and space. He began with the American and French revolutions and took the story to the decolonization movements that resulted in the rise of emerging new nations in Asia and Africa during the 1950s and 1960s. Morris dealt also with the entire world: Europe during "the age of the democratic revolution," throughout the rest of the nineteenth century, and following the two world wars; the emerging countries in the Western hemisphere, especially Latin America in the nineteenth and twentieth centuries; and the new nations of Africa and Asia during the age of anticolonial revolutions in the 1950s and 1960s.

In a brief book Morris could not cover constitutional developments in any depth. His survey, of necessity, was limited and cried for a fuller treatment of many of the important constitutional issues he had raised. The work as a whole, however, should be seen as a serious start toward a more definitive study.[9]

Morris and Palmer in their writings revived a variation of the old Jellinek–Doumergue historiographical controversy. Morris was convinced that the French had copied the Virginia Bill of Rights of 1776 in their Declaration of 1789. "The Virginia statesman George Mason might well have instituted an action of plagiarism against the authors of the Declaration of the Rights of Man and the Citizen which the French National Assembly adopted on August 26, 1789. The resemblance to Mason's Bill of Rights which the Virginia Assembly had enacted back in June of 1776 is too close to be coincidental." Palmer, on the other hand, reproduced the texts of the two documents and, after comparing them, concluded only that there was a "remarkable parallelism." The language of the two documents is, indeed, strikingly similar and supports Palmer's thesis that a community of ideas existed on both sides of the Atlantic. But given the differences in meaning of such words as "liberty," "rights," and "citizen" within the two countries, Palmer's case appears to be the stronger.[10]

One of the most important area studies on the subject was the volume of collected essays, *Constitutionalism in Asia*, that was occasioned by the national program of the Committee on Asian Law during the American Revolution Bicentennial year. Lawrence W. Beer, its editor, was a distinguished scholar in Japanese and comparative constitutional law. What was distinctive about the Beer collection was that each essay was written by an Asian legal scholar or jurist. In terms of cultural relativism, this method marked an improvement over the usual tendency of having American scholars provide the commentary on the influence of American constitutionalism on a given foreign country. The countries covered in this volume included Bangladesh, the Republic of China, India, Indonesia, Japan, Malaysia, the Philippines, and Singapore. The contributors described the constitutional situation not through the tinted glasses of Western legalism, but rather from an indigenous Asian point of view. Beer concluded that the Federal Constitution had a far greater influence on Asian constitutional systems than was generally realized—but that this influence had been determined largely by the Asian countries themselves.[11]

Another book written in the 1970s dealt with one of the most recent developments in the influence of American constitutionalism—the spread of the idea of judicial review. Mauro Cappelletti, who holds positions at Stanford University and the University of Florence, published *Judicial Review in the Contemporary World* in 1971. Although the American idea of judicial review was expounded in the famed *Marbury v. Madison* case, Cappelletti pointed out that the decision could be traced back through a long line of earlier antecedents: origins in ancient

Greece and Rome, the writings of early Church fathers, the ideas of medieval scholastics, actions of French *Parlements*, practices of English courts of equity, the thinking of Enlightenment philosophers, and the judicial experience and background of colonial America. What Cappelletti called the "decentralized" system of judicial control used in America meant that the power of control was to be given to all judicial organs of a given legal system. This American version of judicial review has now spread to many countries of the world. Thus, this feature of American constitutionalism which had been neglected for almost a century and a half, was slowly coming into its own.[12]

A scholarly project of a different nature was written and designed by a team of scholars of the European University Institute in Florence, Italy. Three volumes of this projected multivolume work, *Integration through Law: Europe and the American Federal Experience*—prepared under the general editor, Mauro Cappelletti—appeared in 1985–86. The project, to which nearly forty scholars from numerous countries and three continents contributed, was not designed specifically as a traditional comparative constitutional history. Its main aim was to present a comparative intersystemic legal study to survey the institutions, instrumentalities, and methods of European integration and to compare it with two centuries of American federalism. Many of the essays, nevertheless, contain valuable information and insights into the spread of American constitutionalism in Europe.[13]

Two recent publications treat the spread of American constitutionalism in broad terms. Klaus von Beyme in *America as a Model* seeks to further Friedrich's approach by updating the treatment of certain of his themes from a political science point of view.[14] Albert P. Blaustein has also produced a short paper from a legal perspective, *The Influence of the United States Constitution Abroad*.[15] Besides writing other publications on this subject, Blaustein has also been a scholar-activist and served as a constitutional adviser to several countries—Peru, Bangladesh, Liberia, Zimbabwe, Vietnam, and Korea.

Three important works came to hand too late to be considered in this book. They are: Louis Henkin and Albert Rosenthal, eds., *Constitutionalism and Rights: The Influence of the United States Constitution Abroad*; Mauro Cappelletti, *Judicial Process in Comparative Perspective*; and J. Barton Starr, ed., *The United States Constitution: Its Birth, Growth, and Influence in Asia*. Each has made a significant but selective contribution to the overall subject of the influence of American constitutionalism abroad.[16] Two works are forthcoming: the editor of this volume has under way a study entitled, *Heard Round the World: The Influence of American Constitutionalism Abroad—1776 to Present*; and a book of collected essays, edited by Lawrence W. Beer, to be called *Constitutional Systems in Late Twentieth-Century Asia*.

This bibliographical essay, in summary, has demonstrated one thing: the paucity of broad-ranging scholarly work on this most important subject. Although the topic has been recognized as one worthy of serious attention by several outstanding comparative and legal scholars, it has not been given the prominence it merits nor been studied in the breadth required. Two significant omissions within this book itself immediately come to mind—Canada and Australia—where American constitutional influence played a highly relevant role. Given the creation of so many new nations in Africa since World War II, much work on that continent—an unexplored continent in terms of its comparative constitutional history—remains to be done. Moreover, the creation of new nation-states in central and eastern Europe after World War I—based on the Wilsonian principle of national self-determination—represents another possibility for a fascinating case study. Before a definitive history on the influence of American constitutionalism abroad can be written, studies in depth similar to those found in this volume must be initiated covering the countries of the world.

NOTES

1. Georg Jellinek, *Die Erklärung der Menschen und Bürgerrechte* (Berlin: Duncker and Humblot, 1895); and Max Farrand, trans., *The Declaration of the Rights of Man and of Citizens* (New York: Henry Holt, 1901).

2. Émile Doumergue, "Les Origines historiques de la declaration des droits de l'homme et du citoyen," *Revue du droit public et de la science politique en France et a l'étranger* 21 (1904): 673–733. David G. Ritchie, *Natural Rights* (New York: Macmillan, 1903). For an earlier important statement on this issue see Émile Boutmy, *Études de droit constitutionnel, France, Angleterre, États Unis* (Paris: E Plon, 1885); *Studies in Constitutional Law: France, England, United States*, trans. from the 2nd French edition by Edward Dicey with an Introduction by Albert Dicey (London and New York: Macmillan, 1891). For a fuller bibliographical entry on this controversy over time, see Roland Bainton, "The Appeal to Reason," in Conyers Read, ed., *The Constitution Reconsidered*, revised edition by Richard B. Morris (New York: Harper and Row, 1968) 126–27.

3. Read, ed., *Constitution Reconsidered*, 271–346.

4. Ibid., 297, 343, 333.

5. Hawgood, *Modern Constitutions Since 1787*.

6. Carl J. Friedrich, *Politica Methodice digesta of Johannes Althusius*... (Cambridge, Mass.: Harvard University Press, 1932); and *Constitutional Government and Politics* (New York: Harper and Brothers, 1937).

7. Friedrich, *Impact of American Constitutionalism Abroad*.

8. Palmer, *The Age of the Democratic Revolution*.

9. Morris, *Emerging Nations and the American Revolution*.

10. Ibid., 56; and Palmer, *Age of the Democratic Revolution*, Appendix IV, 1:518–21.

11. Beer, *Constitutionalism in Asia*.

12. Cappelletti, *Judicial Review in the Contemporary World*.

13. Mauro Cappelletti et al., eds., *Integration through Law: Europe and the American Federal Experience* vol. I, books 1, 2, and 3 (Berlin and New York: Walter de Gruyter, 1985–86). For essays most pertinent to the subject at hand, see book 1: Foreword, 3–68, 71–168, 169–243, 244–412, and 603–16; book 2: 3–110, 261–351; and book 3: 3–82, 231–344, and 345–80.

14. Klaus von Beyme, *America as a Model* (New York: St. Martin's Press, 1987).

15. Albert P. Blaustein, *The Influence of the United States Constitution Abroad* (Washington, D.C.: Washington Institute for Values in Public Policy, 1986).

16. Louis Henkin and Albert Rosenthal, eds., *Constitutionalism and Rights: The Influence of the United States Constitution Abroad* (New York: Columbia University

Press, 1990); Mauro Cappelletti, *Judicial Process in Comparative Perspective* (Oxford: Clarendon Press, 1989); and J. Barton Starr, ed., *The United States Constitution: Its Birth, Growth and Influence in Asia* (Hong Kong: Hong Kong University Press, 1988).

Index

About the Contributors

LAWRENCE W. BEER is Fred Morgan Kirby Professor of Civil Rights at Lafayette College. He has written and edited among other books: *The Interplay of Legal Traditions; Human Rights Commissioners and Lay Protection of Human Rights in Japan; A Guide to the Study of Japanese Law; Freedom of Expression in Japan; Constitutionalism in Asia; Constitutional Revolution in Japanese Law, Society and Politics*; and *Constitutional Case Law of Japan.*

GEORGE ATHAN BILLIAS is Jacob and Frances Hiatt Professor of History Emeritus at Clark University. He has written, edited, or co-edited the following books: *Massachusetts Land Bankers of 1740; General John Glover and His Marblehead Mariners; George Washington's Generals; The American Revolution: How Revolutionary Was It?; Law and Authority in Colonial America; Interpretations of American History: Patterns and Perspectives; George Washington's Opponents; The Federalists: Realists or Ideologues?; American History: Retrospect and Prospect; Perspectives on Early American History*; and *Elbridge Gerry: Founding Father and Republican Statesman.*

ROBERT J. KOLESAR, Assistant Professor of History at John Carroll University, is preparing for publication a study to be entitled, *Developing Industrial City: Worcester, Massachusetts in the Late Nineteenth Century.*

NICHOLAS G. ONUF is Professor of Political Science in the School of International Service at American University and has edited *Law-Making in the Global Community*.

PETER S. ONUF is Professor of History at the University of Virginia. He is the author of the following books: *The Origins of the Federal Republic: Jurisdictional Controversies in the United States, 1775–1787; Statehood and Union: A History of the Northwest Ordinance; Maryland and the Empire; Seventeen Seventy-Three: The Antilon-First Citizen Letters*; and co-author of *A Union of Interests: The Political Economy of the Extended Republic*.

WILLIAM SAFRAN, Professor of Political Science at the University of Colorado, is the author of *Veto-Group Politics* and *The French Polity*. He is also co-author of *Comparative Politics: An Introduction to the Politics of the United Kingdom, France, Germany and the Soviet Union*; and *Ideology and Politics: The Socialist Party of France*.

www.ingramcontent.com/pod-product-compliance
Ingram Content Group UK Ltd.
Pitfield, Milton Keynes, MK11 3LW, UK
UKHW020821290926
15470UKWH00003B/1287

9 780313 267574